$14⁹⁵

VG

Ref:: Bibliographies

11.11 E

W9-BRX-252

The Scarecrow Author Bibliographies

1. *A New Steinbeck Bibliography, 1929-1971*, by Tetsumaro Hayashi. 1973.

2. *A Bibliography of Joseph Conrad*, by Theodore G. Ehrsam. 1969.

3. *Arthur Miller Criticism (1930-1967)*, by Tetsumaro Hayashi. 1969.

4. *A Bibliography of the Works of Katherine Anne Porter and of the Criticism of the Works* . . . by Louise Waldrip and Shirley Anne Bauer. 1969.

5. *Freneau's Published Prose: A Bibliography*, by Philip M. Marsh. 1970.

6. *Robert Greene Criticism. A Comprehensive Bibliography*, by Tetsumaro Hayashi. 1971.

7. *Benjamin Disraeli*, by R. W. Stewart. 1972.

8. *John Berryman: A Checklist*, by Richard W. Kelly. 1972.

9. *William Dean Howells: A Bibliography*, by Vito J. Brenni. 1973.

10. *Jean Anouilh: An Annotated Bibliography*, by Kathleen White Kelly. 1973.

11. *E. M. Forster: An Annotated Bibliography of Secondary Materials*, by Alfred Borrello. 1973.

12. *The Marquis de Sade: A Bibliography*, by E. Pierre Chanover. 1973.

13. *Alain Robbe-Grillet: An Annotated Bibliography of Critical Studies, 1953-1972*, by Dale Watson Fraizer. 1973.

14. *Northrop Frye: An Enumerative Bibliography*, by Robert D. Denham. 1974.

15. *The World of Federico García Lorca: A General Bibliographic Survey*, by Joseph L. Laurenti and Joseph Siracusa. 1974.

16. *Ben Jonson: A Quadricentennial Bibliography, 1947-1972*, by D. Heyward Brock and James M. Welsh. 1974.

BEN JONSON:

A Quadricentennial Bibliography, 1947-1972

by

D. Heyward Brock

and

James M. Welsh

The Scarecrow Author Bibliographies, No. 16

The Scarecrow Press, Inc.
Metuchen, N.J.   1974

Library of Congress Cataloging in Publication Data

Brock, Dewey Heyward.
    Ben Jonson: a quadricentennial bibliography, 1947-
1972.

    (The Scarecrow author bibliographies, no. 16)
    1. Jonson, Ben, 1573?-1637--Bibliography. I. Welsh,
James M., joint author.
Z8456.6.B75   016.822'3   74-2424
ISBN 0-8108-0710-6

Copyright 1974 by D. Heyward Brock
and James M. Welsh

CONTENTS

Preface   v

List of Abbreviations Used   viii

INTRODUCTION   11
     Ben Jonson in the Twentieth Century: Some
     Critical Trends

ARTICLES AND NOTES   33

BOOKS AND MONOGRAPHS   95

DISSERTATIONS AND THESES   123

EDITIONS
     Collected and Selected Works   140

     Individual Works: Editions, Adaptations,
       Translations, Textual Commentaries   145

INDEX of Names and Subjects   153

PREFACE

The primary purpose of this book is to provide an up-dated Ben Jonson bibliography for the use of Jonsonian and Renaissance scholars and students. The standard bibliography for Jonson is Samuel A. Tannenbaum's Ben Jonson: A Concise Bibliography (New York, 1938) and (with Dorothy R. Tannenbaum) Supplement to a Concise Bibliography of Ben Jonson (New York, 1947). Together these offer a fairly complete checklist of editions and studies published through mid-1947. Robert C. Steensma's "Ben Jonson: A Checklist of Editions, Biography, and Criticism, 1947-1964" (Research Opportunities in Renaissance Drama, 9 [1966]), augmented by Anthony J. Nania's "Addenda: Ben Jonson: A Checklist of Editions, Biography, and Criticism, 1947-1964" (Research Opportunities in Renaissance Drama, 10 [1967]), is a useful supplement to Tannenbaum, but neither Tannenbaum's checklists nor Steensma's list (augmented by Nania) covers completely the crucial quarter-century between 1947 and 1972. Generally, this period has witnessed a great revival of scholarly interest in Jonson, with perhaps the greatest resurgence occurring from the mid-sixties to the present. Consequently, we have deemed it both desirable and highly appropriate that a bibliography encompassing the major scholarly activity of these years should be published in a single volume during the quadricentennial of Jonson. Since the MLA annual bibliography and abstract system will now presumably be international in scope, we have established 1972 as our terminal date for entries, assuming that scholars and students will be able to use the Jonson items in the MLA annual bibliographies and abstracts to supplement and up-date the present book.

In order to give an overview of Jonsonian scholarship in the twentieth century, we have included an introductory essay which traces some of the most important and influential trends of critical inquiry during the period. In the bibliography itself, we have provided annotations for most of the major books and articles, the content or critical focus

of which may not be clearly discernible from the title. For
many of the more important or less accessible studies, we
have generally given rather extended annotations. For many
of the significant books we have noted at least some of the
major reviews. In treating editions, we have listed major
critical ones; we have made no particular effort to indicate
all of the numerous reprints of Jonson's works. For quick
reference and for the convenience of the user, we have included a names-subjects index at the end of the volume.

The Bibliography is divided into four sections. Section "A" treats "Articles and Notes," and all of the numbered
entries in this section are keyed to the letter "A." Hence,
the notation "A125" in our index will indicate to the user
that this item is an article. Likewise, "B125" would indicate a book, "D125" a dissertation (or thesis), "E125" an
edition. If an essay has appeared as part of a book, it
will be keyed to the anthology under Section "B" ("Books
and Monographs"), not under Section "A" ("Articles and
Notes"), though it would usually also be found under Section "A" if it had first appeared in print in a periodical.
Section "E" ("Editions, Collections, Adaptations," etc.) is
the most highly classified in the book. The section may be
broken down as follows: (1) Collected and Selected Works;
(2) Individual Works: Editions, Adaptations, Translations,
Textual Commentaries. This latter portion is further divided
between prose works and masques and plays. A final word
may be in order for Section "D" ("Dissertations and Theses"),
which is limited to works in English. The M. A. theses
listed (those without designation are doctoral dissertations)
are exclusively British, for we have not attempted to include
those submitted at American and Canadian universities. This
decision was made mainly in the interest of economy and
expediency.

We are indebted to numerous scholars whose labors
over the last twenty-five years have made this Bibliography
possible and necessary. We are also grateful to Mrs.
Betty Sherman, who carefully typed a difficult manuscript
and made many helpful suggestions.

We have attempted to keep the potential reader's
needs and convenience foremost in mind as we designed
and prepared this Bibliography, but, human nature being
what it is, we probably have not been able to include every-
thing that every reader would want or to catch all of the
imperfections which have crept into the work, and for

whatever inconveniences or imperfections still remain in the
book we are solely responsible. Despite its perhaps in-
evitable defects, we hope that those who consult this book
will find it a useful research tool.

D. H. B.
J. M. W.

LIST OF ABBREVIATIONS USED

ArieLE	Ariel: A Review of International English Literature
AUMLA	Journal of the Australasian Universities Language and Literature Association
BA	Books Abroad
BNYPL	Bulletin of the New York Public Library
BRMMLA	Bulletin of the Rocky Mountain Modern Language Association
CE	College English
CL	Comparative Literature
CompD	Comparative Drama
CP	Concerning Poetry (West. Washington St. College)
CR	The Critical Review (Melbourne, Sidney)
E&S	Essays and Studies by Members of the English Association
EIC	Essays in Criticism
ELH	English Literary History
ELN	English Language Notes
ELR	English Literary Renaissance
EM	English Miscellany
ES	English Studies
ETJ	Educational Theatre Journal
EWR	East-West Review (Doshisha Univ., Kyoto, Japan)
Expl	Explicator
GorR	The Gordon Review (Wenham, Mass.)

HAB	Humanities Association Bulletin (Canada)
HLQ	Huntington Library Quarterly
HudR	Hudson Review
JEGP	Journal of English and Germanic Philology
JHI	Journal of the History of Ideas
JWCI	Journal of the Warburg and Courtauld Institute
KR	Kenyon Review
MLN	Modern Language Notes
MLQ	Modern Language Quarterly
MLR	Modern Language Review
MP	Modern Philology
N&Q	Notes and Queries
NEQ	New England Quarterly
NM	Neuphilologische Mitteilungen
PLL	Papers on Language and Literature
PMLA	Publications of the Modern Language Association of America
PQ	Philological Quarterly
Q	quarto
QJS	Quarterly Journal of Speech
QQ	Queen's Quarterly
RenD	Renaissance Drama
RenQ	Renaissance Quarterly
RES	Review of English Studies
RN	Renaissance News
SAQ	South Atlantic Quarterly
SB	Studies in Bibliography: Papers of the Bibliographical Society of the Univ. of Virginia
SCN	Seventeenth-Century News
SCr	Strumenti Critici (Torino)
SEL	Studies in English Literature
ShN	Shakespeare Newsletter

ShS	Shakespeare Survey
ShStud	Shakespeare Studies (Japan)
SJ	Shakespeare Jahrbuch
SJW	Shakespeare-Jahrbuch (Weimar)
SP	Studies in Philology
SQ	Shakespeare Quarterly
SR	Studies in the Renaissance
TLS	Times [London] Literary Supplement
TSL	Tennessee Studies in Literature
TSLL	Texas Studies in Language and Literature
UMSE	Univ. of Mississippi Studies in English
UTQ	Univ. of Toronto Quarterly
YWES	Year's Work in English Studies

INTRODUCTION

Ben Jonson in the Twentieth Century:
Some Critical Trends

An overview of Jonsonian criticism in the first seven
decades of the twentieth century is not easily achieved, but
there are discernible trends that have developed and branched
off in divergent directions, following the critical signposts of
the times. Some of these critical paths are better laid than
others; some are more direct and decidedly well-paved;
others are circuitous and labyrinthine, beset with obstacles
and therefore rather challenging; still others have fallen to
neglect although the routes they take may still have a certain
scenic and sentimental charm. Yet most of these paths
point in the same general direction--the common destination
being a better understanding of one of the supreme poetic
talents of an era.

The reception of Ben Jonson in the twentieth century
was to no small extent influenced by criticism that originated
in the latter decades of the nineteenth century. In general,
since the publication of A.C. Swinburne's critical study of
Ben Jonson in 1889, scholars, many of them no doubt stimulated by the inadequacies of Swinburne's work, have produced
critical studies of Jonson's artistic temperament (particularly
in contrast to and in praise of Shakespeare's), his dramatic
and poetic theory and practice, and, most prolifically, his
classicism. [1] For the most part, critics have adjudged Jonson's artistic temperament to be overly intellectual, more
Roman and Stoic than English and Christian; his dramatic
and poetic theory to be essentially derivative from Terence,
Plautus, Aristotle, and Horace; his artistic craftmanship to
be arduous and labored; his poetic works to be decorous and
well-constructed but heavy-handed and stiff; and his classicism, except in the profundity of its influence, to be beyond
question and fundamentally pervasive in all of his artistic
endeavors. Fortunately, in the last four decades much
Jonsonian scholarship has successfully attempted, and in

11

many cases is still in the process of trying, to modify these
evaluations; but, on the whole, the critical image of Jonson
that yet remains too firmly imprinted is that of the labored
artificer who cannot sing and the heavy-handed adapter of the
classics who looks backwards to the Golden Age and remains
aloof from his own.

With their interest in poets who were inspired by the
divine afflatus and thus who could sing sweetly and spontane-
ously and dramatists who portrayed individualized characters,
not types, with few notable exceptions, the late nineteenth-
century critics did not find Jonson an artist to their liking,
although they admired him for his vast learning. In Jonson's works, nineteenth-century critics did not discover the
characteristics of the great poet or, as they liked to call
him, the true singer--melodic verse, a focus upon the
poet's own individuality, the spontaneous overflow of powerful feelings, and an inspired, unconscious creativity. In
his study first published in the English Worthies series in
1886, J. A. Symonds argued that Jonson's artistic temperament was fundamentally and originally romantic but that it
had been "overlaid and diverted from its spontaneous bias
by a scholar's education and by definite theories of the poet's
task, deliberately adopted and tenaciously adhered to in middle life."[2] Similarly, A. C. Swinburne found Jonson's greatest fault in his inability to sing and to create sympathy for
his characters,[3] and his greatest merit in the sententious-
ness of his Discoveries. Although admiring Jonson as a
great scholar and even a great writer, but not a great poet,
Swinburne concluded that

> The case of Ben Jonson is the great standing ex-
> ample of a truth which should never be forgotten
> or overlooked; that no amount of learning, of
> labour, or of culture will supply the place of
> natural taste and native judgement--will avail in
> any slightest degree to confer the critical faculty
> upon a man to whom nature has denied it. Just
> judgement of others, just judgement of himself,
> was all but impossible to this great writer, this
> consummate and indefatigable scholar, this gener-
> ous and enthusiastic friend.[4]

Just two years before the turn of the century, two
other significant critical works appeared. F. E. Schelling's
article on Jonson's classicism is still considered a seminal
work on the subject. Comparing Spenserian and Jonsonian

poetic styles and temperaments, Schelling found Jonson's
poetic manner to be essentially "assimilative" of classical
qualities and the classics. He proposed that Jonson's "assimilative classicism" was reflected in his choice of subject, especially in the poet's preference for "applied poetry over
pure poetry"; in his treatment of the subject, particularly
with regard to the sense of design and construction; in his
diction, anticipating those characteristics of the coming neo-
classical period in English literature (such as care in word
choice, slightly Latinized vocabulary, and the use of paral-
lelism); and, finally, in his versification, showing a strong
preference for the decasyllabic couplet unlike Spenser but
quite similar to Waller, Dryden, and Pope. [5] Appearing also
in 1898, Elisabeth Woodbridge's Studies in Jonson's Comedies
contended, unlike Schelling's study, that Jonson's classicism
was not a question of borrowing or assimilation as such, but
a question of what Jonson himself perceived as truth. Woodbridge argued cogently that Jonson's classicism was not a
result of a completely blind devotion to the classics, but the
result of a devotion to truth as he discerned it, not devotion
to a convention or tradition, because Jonson

> claimed the right of free thought in the realm of
> letters as others had claimed it in the domain of
> religion, and if he made few departures from
> classic practice this was because he had given to
> the classic standards his independent and deliberate
> assent. It was with him a question not of authori-
> ties but of truth. [6]

Significant twentieth-century criticism of Jonson began
in 1907 with the publication of Maurice Castelain's exhaustive
Ben Jonson: L'Homme et l'oeuvre. Although jocularly sug-
gesting that Jonson's greatest fault was being a contemporary
of Shakespeare, Castelain declared that Jonson's classicism
was impure and that he was essentially English in temperament and the embodiment of the man of action. If one
studies Jonson carefully, without always arbitrarily resorting
to what Castelain considered a ridiculous and unnecessary
comparison to Shakespeare, one comes to understand and to
appreciate both the worth and beauty of Jonson the man and
his art.

> Il y a pourtant dans son oeuvre une certaine part
> d'originalité que nous avons essayé de définir et
> qu'il ne faut pas déprécier; il y a surtout une
> puissance d'honnêteté qu'on ne peut s'empêcher

d'admirer. L'homme et l'écrivain ont eu des
défauts, non pas de ces 'heureux défauts' pour
lesquels le monde est très volontiers indulgent;
mais à vivre longtemps dans l'intimité de son
oeuvre et de sa personne, notre estime de l'une
et de l'autre n'ont fait que s'accroître. [7]

Following Castelain's lead, G. G. Smith also attempted to
encourage appreciation for Jonson's virtues of honesty, self
reliance, and crafted artistry, and to divert attention from
his faults of harshness, pugnacity, and egotism. [8] But, like
the late nineteenth-century critics, Smith contended that Jonson's stiffness in verse and his weighted intellectualism that
neglected emotion led to his difficulties in achieving true
greatness as a poet.

Preceding the publication of the first volumes of the
Herford and Simpson Oxford edition of Jonson's works in
1925, perhaps the most influential and perceptive contribution
to Jonsonian studies was T. S. Eliot's essay appearing in
1919. In that study Eliot asserted that Jonson's poetry is
difficult for us to appreciate because it is "poetry of the
surface, " and "poetry of the surface cannot be understood
without study; for to deal with the surface of life, as Jonson
dealt with it, is to deal so deliberately that we too must be
deliberate, in order to understand. "[9] But Eliot also realized
that because of the nature of Jonson's artistic appeal, his
audience and those who genuinely appreciate him would probably never be numerous:

The immediate appeal of Jonson is to the mind; his
emotional tone is not in the single verse, but in
the design of the whole. But not many people are
capable of discovering for themselves the beauty
which is only found after labor; and Jonson's in-
dustrious readers have been those whose interest
was historical and curious, and those who have
thought that in discovering the historical and curious interest they had discovered the artistic value
as well. When we say that Jonson requires study,
we do not mean study of his classical scholarship
or of seventeenth century manners. We mean in-
telligent saturation in his work as a whole; we
mean that in order to enjoy him at all, we must
get to the center of his work and his temperament,
and that we must see him unbiased by time, as a
contemporary. And to see him as a contemporary

does not so much require the power of putting our-
selves into seventeenth century London as it requires the power of seeing Jonson in our London.[10]

What finally impressed Eliot most profoundly about Jonson as
an artist was his fine sense of form and his sense for what
Eliot called the living art.

Within eighteen years after Eliot's essay, three important studies of Jonson appeared. In his essay on Jonson's
lyric poetry, R. S. Walker contended, echoing Eliot, that
Jonson was perhaps the first Englishman to have a clear
conception of art as a living process, dependent for its wel-
fare on the service and devotion of its practitioners. Walker also called for a critical "depersonalization" of Jonson
if we are to approach him in a frame of mind free from ir-
relevant preconceptions about the personality of the man.
Only in Jonson, Walker argued, do we find a complete ab-
sorption and indefinable spirit indicated by the term classical,
but we do not gauge his classicism accurately by uncovering
his sources, for Jonson's whole development as a literary
artist resolves itself into a huge struggle to give utterance
to the peculiar harmony which he felt within himself between
emotional inspiration and intellectual conviction, a struggle
which consequently produced a sensibility radically different
from any previously expressed in English literature. What
Jonsonian criticism needs to do, Walker insisted, is to
evaluate the originality of Jonson's lyric sensibility for what
it is, and simply because that has not been done explains
why so little genuine criticism of Jonson has appeared.[11]

First published in 1934, John Palmer's critical biography of Jonson provided an excellent example of the kind
of Jonsonian criticism that Walker was attacking in his article. What interested Palmer about Jonson was the artist's
inability to express a sweet singing of the spirit and the
seeming insincerity of Jonson's religious convictions. Proclaiming Jonson a pagan Stoic who merely spoke in Christian
phrases, Palmer declared,

That [Jonson] professed the Catholic or Anglican
conventions was neither here nor there. There is
no deep sense of spiritual issues anywhere in his
plays. These poems of devotion are a pious exercise, of interest only as showing how even the
most powerful and independent minds, can honestly
subscribe to doctrines without allowing them

seriously to affect their conduct or vital concerns. [12]

With his study of drama and society in Jonson's age,
L. C. Knights made a valuable contribution to dramatic
scholarship and suggested a meaningful new approach to the
study of Jonson. Proclaiming Jonson the greatest of the
dramatists who handled social themes, Knights found Jonson's greatness springing not from his unique qualities but
from a common ground which he shared with his contemporaries and which was represented by certain beliefs or
attitudes concerning the relative worth and dignity of human
desires. Knights contended that "in his handling of ambi-
tion, greed, lust, acquisitiveness, and so on he implicitly,
but clearly, refers to a more than personal scheme of values. Jonson in short was working in a tradition."[13] Primarily concerned with defining the nature of that tradition
and its effect on Jonson, Knights demonstrated that the basic
economic pattern of the Elizabethan and Stuart periods, a
pattern inherited from the Middle Ages but superimposed
upon by the design of capitalistic enterprise, was highly influential in the development of Jonson's thematic considera-
tions in his plays.

Significant Jonsonian scholarship during and shortly
after World War II centered around the question of Jonson's
artistic qualifications and the nature of his art. In his essay published in 1944 on Jonson's art, Percy Simpson
sounded a familiar note by proclaiming Jonson's outlook on
life to be ruthlessly intellectual, but Simpson extolled Jonson
for originality in his dramatic plots, his artistic ideal of
balance, his sane and well-constructed work, and the "scru-
pulous fineness of his literary conscience" and the "fibre of
his English manhood."[14] A year later G. B. Johnston published the only extensive study to that date which dealt exclusively with Jonson as a poet and with an analysis of his
poetry. Johnston demonstrated that Jonson's art was primarily an outgrowth of the native tradition and was informed
essentially by the vital observation of contemporary life, although his art obviously assimilated the classics to advan-
tage, principally by didacticizing them. According to Johnston, Jonson's ability to make traditional material sound
deeply personal makes him a great poet and, at the same
time, leads to his being misinterpreted because critics too
frequently find biography in lines "which may be the product
of moods only or of traditions assimilated and applied per-
sonally."[15] Jonson was a great poet, Johnston concluded,

because he

> caught a vision of the glories of learning and im-
> bibed an abhorrence of ignorance. His passionate-
> ly held respect for truth, a keen sense of fact,
> and shaping imagination which stamped even chaos
> with form combined to drive him into the other
> world of poetry. There he found the truth, the
> order, the beauty, and the justice which he could
> not find in his London. In poets dead and living
> he met peers more admirable and more congenial
> than he found either among the proudest nobles of
> England or the 'many-headed Bench.' Associated
> with the poets he must have felt himself part of
> the stream of creation which flows through time
> from generation to generation. For like all true
> poets he is a summary of what has gone before
> and a prophecy of what is to follow. In him meet
> the classics, the Middle Ages, and the Renaissance,
> and (what has been far less generally realized) the
> principal trends of English literature of the three
> centuries following his death. [16]

H. W. Baum's study published in 1947 claimed that
Jonson merely employed didacticism for literary and dramatic
purposes and that he was not in any strict sense either
moralist, sociologist, economist, or reformer. Since, according to Baum, Jonson accepted the broad and inclusive
Renaissance theory of the high function of the poet in society,
his own theory of art was neither narrow nor strictly moral-
istic, and his attack on the follies and vices of his age was
"rooted in intellectual and rational rather than moral and
emotional standards." Jonson saw poetry as "the eternal
voice of men's best visions" that acted "positively and directly upon society as the most powerful force for its better-
ment. Dramatic poetry he practiced with a keen sense of
his responsibility."[17] Appearing in the same year as
Baum's study, F. L. Townsend's analysis of Jonson's art
argued that the completely classical Jonson is merely a fig-
ment of critical imaginations and that Jonson's greatest
dramatic successes are those, as especially in the case of
Bartholomew Fair, in which he is least classical and in
which the careful ordering of his materials, the rich variety,
and the ingenius weaving together of his manifold "comic
threads" are most apparent.[18] Two years after Townsend's
study, L. J. Potts went even further in attempting to show
Jonson's independence of the classics and his kinship with

his own age by contending that the rigid texture and structure of Jonson's plays reveal not a slavish imitation of the
classics but a determined effort to make literature conform
to the new philosophy, especially to the theory of art advo-
cated by Francis Bacon.[19]

By the middle of the twentieth century, although many
reputable critics--such as Douglas Bush[20] and Cleanth Brooks
and W. K. Wimsatt[21]--were still proclaiming to agreeing
ears Jonson's heavy indebtedness to the classics and were
emphasizing his labored artistry, significant progress had
been made in the attempt to relieve Jonson from the burden
of the classics and to establish the independence of his artistic theory and practice. In a brilliantly perceptive, but
unfortunately, it would seem, not overly influential essay,
Louis I. Bredvold argued for the indigenous nature of English neo-classicism in general and Jonson's classicism in
particular; and, declaring Jonson as English as John Bull
despite all of his learning, Bredvold urged careful study of
the varied manifestations of the classical spirit in English
literature and especially careful study of the organism that
assimilates the classical spirit, for "it is the organism that
assimilates the influence which must be understood in all its
individuality, its native tendencies, its past history as well
as its present condition. Only the influence which is thus
assimilated is really worth studying."[22]

Actually, the decade following the publication of Bredvold's essay did see a critical de-emphasis of Jonson's
classicism and a concentration on his individuality. In 1950
Bertril Johansson published his disappointingly uncritical
study of Jonson's religion and superstition.[23] A year later,
Eugene M. Waith called attention to Jonson's concern with
the moral responsibility of the poet,[24] and in 1952 K. M.
Burton pointed out that Jonson's political tragedies are concerned with the tragic flaw within the social order rather
than the individual.[25] In 1953 Marchette Chute published
an interesting but uncritical biography of Jonson's rather
colorful life.[26] In 1953 also Maurice Hussey attempted to
define more thoroughly Jonson's moral and religious standards as reflected in his plays.[27] Following suit, John S.
Weld argued in 1954 that Volpone is really a decidedly
Christian satirical comedy on the theme of the folly of
worldliness.[28] In 1957 H. R. Hays argued that Jonson
thought of himself primarily as a dramatic satirist whose
function was to try to make the spectator face the dark
depths of himself, drag them out into the open, and laugh
at them, thus achieving a kind of moral catharsis.[29] In the

same year John J. Enck analyzed Jonson's comic truth and
found it to be characterized by follies based on contemporary
foibles, characters reduced to simplified drives, a neatly
turned conclusion, and clarity throughout and by a groping
after realism that had to penetrate "more deeply than the
shallow soil of Jacobean society."[30] Appearing one year
before J. B. Bamborough's superficial and uncritical study
of Jonson,[31] Edward B. Partridge's important study analyzed Jonson's metaphorical language and artistic method in
the major comedies and attempted thereby to reveal how his
imagination worked. According to Partridge, Jonson explored, like all comic poets, the disparity between what men
say and what they do, and he dramatized this discrepancy by
inverting in his comedies the values "which are commonly
accepted and made those inverted values the real values of
the world which he dramatically created."[32]

     Since 1960 much Jonsonian scholarship has either ex-
plored Jonson's artistic method or the nature of his poetry
and drama. Jonas A. Barish has offered an exhaustive
study of Jonson's language of prose comedy and has argued
that Jonson's prose is a monumental achievement "in the way
it gives definitive shape to one aspect of the language of a
generation, and makes that language not merely an adjunct
of comedy, but comedy itself."[33] Barish concluded that "if
linguistic realism is a valuable artistic technique, no playwright before Jonson copied live speech more tellingly, and
few since have more powerfully worked it into a design that
transcends mere realism."[34] Analyzing Elizabethan life and
literature as reflected in Jonson's art, Esther C. Dunn's
study first published in 1925 but reissued in 1963 contended
that Jonson's comic sense was apart and overhead and looked
down upon life and revealed it to the world delicately dis-
torted by his intellectual and moral concerns, in order to
emphasize to his audience the follies of his day.[35] In his
analysis of the arguments of Jonson's plays, C. G. Thayer
decided that the early plays explore the details of the vices
and follies of men on the Jonsonian assumption that men and
society could correct their vices and follies through laughter;
the best plays, however, are directed, usually it would ap-
pear unsuccessfully, at a small segment of the population.[36]
In his introduction to Jonson's drama, Robert E. Knoll contended that the plays are more indigenous than classical and
that those which are most successful are the ones that em-
ploy native, Christian stories,[37] a position which provides a
curious contrast to Jackson I. Cope's contention that Bartholomew Fair is a blasphemy, in which Jonson has "blas-

phemed the Scriptures and denied the very omnipotence of
God himself. "[38] In 1965 and 1966 appeared two other important studies of Jonson's dramatic works, the masques in
this particular case, both of which attempt to demonstrate
the poetic quality of the Jonsonian masque, Stephen Orgel's
study[39] unconvincingly and John C. Meagher's[40] cogently,
but with perhaps an overemphasis on the Platonic influence
upon Jonson's thought.

In many respects during the sixties and early seven-
ties, Jonson's plays have consistently stimulated the most
lively and diverse criticism. In 1962 Eugene Waith suggested that Bartholomew Fair is one of the "clearest examples of the survival in the Elizabethan public theater of
the essentially medieval tradition of staging. "[41] Eight years
later R. B. Parker argued that the play was also influenced
by the emblematic tradition, so that "the puppet show is
within a fair which is within a bear-baiting theatre, which
is within a greedy, quarrelsome, childish world; and Jonson,
like the superb stage artist he is, explores their analogies
with his theatre, his company, and his particular, popular
audience constantly in mind. "[42] In his essay on the play,
John M. Potter contended that Jonson developed the structure
of the play around certain elements and themes of Old Comedy in an attempt to adapt the form of Old Comedy to the
Jacobean stage. [43] In analyzing the major plays, John T.
French discovered what he termed Jonson's "aesthetic of
relief" and concluded that Jonson did "have something like a
philosophical development which he refused to push beyond
the humanistic formula of his concept of art. "[44] In his important essay, L. A. Beaurline argued that the illusion of
completeness Jonson achieved in his major plays is influenced by the idea of an infinite class, so that "Jonson's
comic plots are like the working out of a series of permuta-
tions with a fixed number of constants and one variable. "[45]
According to Thomas M. Greene, the associations of the
circle provide the key to understanding Jonson's plays as
well as his other works, [46] while Daniel C. Boughner has
attempted, rather unimpressively, to demonstrate Jonson's
indebtedness to Machiavelli in dramatic theory and in political ideas. [47]

Sounding the classical note again, Colburn Gum has
argued rather convincingly that Jonson was more influenced
by Aristophanes than has previously been recognized, and
he has concluded that Jonson did not follow Aristophanes and
Old Comedy strictly but rather selected certain "features

for adaptation and imitation, but never forsook the examples
of Plautus and Terence."[48]   Alan Dessen, on the other hand,
has concluded that "Jonson's great plays alchemize the base
metal of the allegorical-didactic dramatic tradition into a
unique form that can stand in opposition to the disorder and
anarchy of his contemporary society."[49]   Calling Jonson's
plays "drama of revelation," Gabriele Jackson has cogently
examined the way in which the combination of vision and
judgment operates in the plays and makes them great.   She has
explained that Jonson's plays present

> ... vision in the framework and judgment in the
> specific content, while at the end judgment on the
> characters turns into vision by them.   Jonson's
> audience, too, is included in the central dichotomy.
> He sees them as having an instinctive moral and
> aesthetic responsiveness which is analogous to the
> poet's faculty of vision and which grasps the poet's
> non-logical devices of action and language, by
> which the audience, in turn, is enabled to judge
> rightly both characters and framework.   The trans-
> mission of absolute truths thus depends upon an
> unbroken chain of alternating vision and judgment:
> the poet as visionary perceives what is ultimately
> true; by the use of his aesthetic judgment he con-
> structs a play the total working of which (composed
> of framework-vision and content-judgment) will
> constitute a vision--that is, a revelation--for his
> audience; his audience apprehends this revelation
> through its own faculty of ethical and aesthetic
> vision (which enables it to make appropriate judg-
> ments on the action); having apprehended it, the
> audience is to judge its own behavior against the
> perceived vision. [50]

Claiming that Jonson is now coming into his own as
one of the great dramatists of the English Renaissance, Joe
Lee Davis has attempted to provide a critical guide to the
rather heterogeneous group of minor dramatists in Caroline
England who wrote popular plays in the Jonsonian vein of
comedy.[51]   In his perceptive study, W. David Kay has re-
examined Jonson's early plays with special attention to the
way in which they reflect the deliberate shaping and the
progress of Jonson's literary career and the establishment
for himself of a public identity as a serious poet.[52]   With
some degree of success, Larry S. Champion has recon-
sidered Jonson's late plays and argued that they should not

be termed the 'dotages' of a 'washed-out brain,' for "although the effecting of a comic intent in each of the late
plays differs markedly, the demand on a rationale and the
impetus to explore are as powerful as ever."[53] Since Jonson never left a complete treatise on his critical theory,
James D. Redwine, Jr., has assembled a useful volume of
Jonson's literary criticism gleaned from throughout his
works.[54]

The major comedies and even the tragedies have con-
tinued to provoke varied critical reaction. In 1969 Myrddin
Jones proclaimed that the caricature of Sir Epicure Mammon
in the Alchemist implies that he is Anti-Christ and as such
would have been recognized and condemned by the contemporary audience,[55] while Judd Arnold argued that the triumph
of Lovewit in the play suggests that Jonson was "not com-
mitted to the general reform of mankind," but to "applaud-
ing and enjoying the personal triumph of the cavalierly aloof,
intellectual aristocrat over the hopeless mass of fools."[56]
In his study of the prose paradox and Epicoene, William
Slights observed that "as moral attitudes become more
closely integrated with artistic form in the plays, punishment serves increasingly as emotional resolution rather than
as the execution of strict justice."[57] In attempting to identify ethical values in Volpone, C. J. Gianakaris concluded
that "sound, reasonable conduct" epitomizes the values within the play,[58] and Harriet Hawkins asserted that in the play,
"as in the Praise of Folly, the deceivers who are deceived
ultimately themselves are presented as fit objects for the
diversion and (by way of it) the instruction of rational
men."[59] Gerald H. Cox III has seen Jonson's indebtedness
to medieval cycles in his treatment of Celia and Bonario in
a manner which is "remarkably similar to that of the sacred
figures in the Corpus Christi plays."[60]

Although often considered failures, both of Jonson's
tragedies have inspired interesting commentary during the
last few years. In her analysis of Catiline, Angela G.
Dorenkamp has contended that if history is the shaping spirit
of the play, then Jonson should not be "tried in the court of
Aristotle, or Seneca, or Horace, or Shakespeare," but
rather the play should be viewed as "an extension of the
scope of history."[61] To date, the most fascinating, although not very convincing, major study of Catiline has been
that of B. N. De Luna in which she has attempted to demonstrate that the play was both "intended and in some circles
understood as a classical parallelograph on the Gunpowder

Plot of 1605. "[62] The "antitragic character" of Sejanus,
Arthur F. Marotti has contended, is "shaped largely by Jonson's over-indulgence in self-conscious artifice, "[63] but, in
his examination of the play in terms of the tradition of the
ideal prince, K. W. Evans has found that Sejanus is a "bril-
liant satire on the struggle for power and the trends towards
despotism in Jacobean England. "[64]

Much of the major criticism in the last ten years
has also concerned itself, although not abundantly, with the
previously neglected part of the Jonsonian canon, namely the
poetry. Calling attention to this critical neglect in 1962,
Geoffrey Walton attempted a limited approach to an appreciation of the poetry by analyzing its characteristic tone. He
found Jonson's tone to be dignified and courteous and contended that Jonson's poetry, "even more than his plays,
links seventeenth-century culture and the polite civilization
to the Augustans and to the better features of the medieval
social order and to the half-religious ideal of courtesy. "[65]
Following Walton's lead, Paul M. Cubeta studied Jonson's
religious lyrics and discovered that they were greatly influenced by the medieval and Renaissance religious medita-
tive exercises of such men as St. Bernard of Clairvaux and
St. Ignatius Loyola. [66] In his study of the poetry, Rufus D.
Putney emphasized that the poetry as a whole reveals almost
as much Biblical influence as classical, [67] and Charlotte
Winzeler later argued that Jonson's poetry reflects the fusion
of classical and his own Elizabethan thought, especially
Christian thought, and pointed out that a seemingly pagan
poem like "An Execration Upon Vulcan" is structured around
a prayer form of the Elizabethan Anglican Church. [68] In
analyzing the Christian wisdom of "On My First Sonne, " W.
David Kay argued that the simplicity of language in the poem,
as in Jonson's poetry as a whole, should not be mistaken for
simplicity of thought and that, in order to clarify Jonson's
religious perspective on human love, the poem should be
read in the light of certain analogous passages from the
works of St. Augustine. [69] Not all recent studies of the
poetry have de-emphasized the classical influence on Jonson.
Providing a notable example, Wesley Trimpi examined Jonson's poetic style and argued, in a study perhaps too limited by its thesis to be significantly perceptive, that Jonson
was indebted for his poetic style to certain ancient writers
but primarily to the neo-Latin authorities for the plain style,
authorities such as Erasmus, Vives, and Lipsius. [70]

Published in 1969, J. G. Nichols' eclectic and im-

pressionistic study of Jonson's poems added little new to our
understanding of the techniques of Jonson's verse, [71] but the
book reflected a modern appreciation for Jonson's poetry,
the genuine value of which many contemporaries have considered only as curiously antiquarian. But several contemporary scholars have made attempts to evaluate the peculiar
poetic quality of Jonson's verse. In his study of pastoral
and counterpastoral, Raymond Williams stated that Jonson's
poems celebrating a rural order are an extraction of the
curse of labor by the power of art: "a magical recreation
of what can be seen as a natural beauty and then a willing
charity: each serving to ratify and bless the country land-
owner, or, by a characteristic reification, his house. Yet
this extraction of the curse of labour is in fact achieved by
a simple extraction of the existence of labourers. "[72] Contending that Jonson is an "artistic schizophrenic, " Arthur F.
Marotti described Jonson's poetry as ranging between the
"extremes of copiousness and restraint" and focused his
analysis on essentially two kinds of Jonsonian verse: "the
first a poetry of explosive imagery and perverse imagining,
the second a poetry of more visible control, imagistically
spare, prosodically tight, and intellectually lucid. "[73] Declaring that a Jonsonian poem is a "highly wrought artifact"
in which the linguistic texture is "activated by what on the
surface appears to be an imperfection of one kind or other, "
William V. Spanos claimed that a Jonson poem is "jarred
into motion, thus rendering original what appears to be conventional, spontaneous what appears to be imitative, subtle
what appears to be simple, and, above all, alive what appears to be inanimate. "[74]

   From the critical views summarized thus far emerge
two predominant positions with implications of particular interest to those scholars who have investigated Jonson's social ideals. If, as a number of the critics have argued,
Jonson's artistic temperament is essentially classical and
intellectual, then we may indeed view his social outlook as
fundamentally historical and aloof from the social ideals and
concerns of his own age and his works as platitudinous em-
bodiments of classical ideals and theory; that is to say, the
understanding of Jonson as a pure classicist who looks backwards to the ideals of a past age and whose works merely
restate and idealize the values of classicism is correct. If
such is the case, then his poetic works cannot be seen as
vital and expressive of universal values, as great poetic
works always are, but merely as curious pieces in the history of English literature. On the other hand, if Jonson's

temperament is essentially assimilative of those elements of classicism which have universal value and his fundamental inspiration is not classicism per se, but truth wherever he discovers it, then we may not accurately view him as simply aloof from his own age and from his own indigenous intellectual and social environment, and we may well discover that his works provide a significant and vital evaluation of his own society in the light of traditional ideals drawn from classical, medieval, and, perhaps even, Renaissance sources. If such is the case, then we need, as several critics have implied, to reevaluate the poet who has assimilated his experience and learning and to attempt an understanding of his works, not as the products of a classicist, but as the products of a poet who, like any great poet, assimilates those ideals which have preceded him and those which surround him, and anticipates those which will follow him.

A few critics have partially attempted to fulfill this need by touching upon Jonson's social views. This brief survey of the major currents of Jonsonian criticism for about the last dozen decades has thus far neglected, with few exceptions (notably Knight's seminal work), to mention another significant, although thus far only inadequately explored, current of criticism, namely that concerned with the social nature of Jonson's poetry and drama. Besides Knights, several other critics have at least observed that a strong social concern and influence does seem to be apparent in Jonson's poetry and drama. Calling his drama the first and perhaps the only triumph of social realism on the English stage, Julian Symmes argued in 1940 that Jonson failed as a dramatist because he attempted to be both social satirist and realist at the same time. Symmes pointed out that Jonson was passionately interested in society, in the way people around him lived and moved, but, unlike most social-realistic dramatists, Jonson was not interested, so Symmes believed, in employing his drama as a means of effecting social reform, but only in the dramatic possibilities of, say, a news office or a fair.[75] Writing nine years after Symmes, L. J. Potts contended that the important feature of Jonson's comedy of humors was

> his firm grasp of the notion of eccentricity, which inspired the measurement of everyone against a natural norm; and his sound instinct in linking this notion with comedy, which is society's most effective weapon against the contrary and anarchical tendencies in human nature. This enabled him to

raise comedy to the level of a serious criticism
of life, different in aim and character from tragedy, but not inferior. [76]

In their studies, both H. W. Baum and Eugene M.
Waith called attention to the seriousness with which Jonson took
his intellectual and moral responsibility to society as a
poet, [77] and H. R. Hays indicated the social cathartic effect
of Jonson's best dramatic satire. [78] The articles of K. M.
Burton and Michael J. C. Echeruo, both concerned with the
tragedies, emphasized, respectively, Jonson's awareness of
the tragic implication for individuals effected by corrupted
and flawed societies and his strong sense of and profound
concern with the political conscience. [79]

Several important critical studies have also com-
mented on the social aspects of the poetry. In his analysis
of "To Penshurst, " G. R. Hibbard observed that the social
structure implicit in the poem recognizes the importance of
a place for everyone in the life of the community and especially for the poet, whose function it is to make the society significantly aware of itself and to promote the proper
employment of all of its resources--human, animate, and inanimate. [80] Jeffrey Hart analyzed this idea in more detail
in his essay on "To Penhurst" and argued that Jonson, as
the poet in the poem, was secure in his place at Penshurst
because the social function of poetry was clearly recognized;
"the poet was the moral instructor of the governing class, "[81]
and thus helped to promote the idea that culture is trans-
mitted through the family. The order of Penshurst, Hart
explained, no matter how just or natural it may be, entails
"self-sacrifice and some pain. " In his study of "To Penshurst, " Paul M. Cubeta also emphasized the necessity for
recognizing that perhaps more than any other poet of his age
Jonson must be understood as a moral and social critic as
well as a man of letters. In explaining Jonson's artistic
technique, Cubeta contended that "Jonson's technique for defining his personal and social ethics is to establish the ideal,
whether it be a moral value, a noble character, or a Uto-
pian world, in sharp contrast with the empirical reality of
the world he lives in. "[82] According to G. A. E. Parfitt,
what makes Jonson's poetry distinctive is the centrality of
a consistent ethical position which is socially rather than
religiously biased. [83] In his discussion of the Epigrammes,
David Wykes pointed out that in these poems, as in almost
all of his others, Jonson is concerned primarily with morals
and society, so that the persons praised in the epigrams are

intended to act as moral exemplars for the reader. [84]

    To date, Hugh Maclean's essay on Jonson's ordered society as reflected in the poetry is the most extensive treatment of this subject. He contended that, although the plays deal primarily with those elements which contribute to social disorder, the poetry, even though not providing an explicit and detailed outline of the social order Jonson admired, does reflect "notes" on the particular elements that ought to indicate a society properly ordered, as well as suggestions for right conduct in the midst of a disordered society. Maclean's conclusion is worth quoting as a representative summary of the present skeletal status of the critical discussion of Jonson's social concerns in his poetry:

> In brief, the poems lay stress on the virtue of friendship between good men, who are receptive by nature to the free exchange of opinion and counsel, and on the strong resource such friendships constitute for the ordered society and the secure state. They reflect also Jonson's views on the relationship that ought ideally to obtain between prince and poet, in the interest of the people at large. Finally, they indicate the social attitudes and actions befitting a 'ruling class' which thoroughly understands the nature of its responsibility and desires to make them effective. [85]

    As can be seen from the preceding discussion of critical trends, Jonsonian scholarship thus far in the twentieth century has reassessed many old avenues of critical inquiry and has explored several new ones. The increased scholarly interest in Jonson in the last two decades especially seems to indicate that scholars have, in their own way, rediscovered the richness, the variety, and the unique character of Jonson the man and of Jonson the poet, the dramatist, the masque writer, the essayist, the literary critic, and the literary monarch. Despite the progress Jonsonian criticism has made in the twentieth century, much work still remains to be done: the definitive critical biography is yet to be written, Jonson's classicism and his humanism still need to be clarified, Jonson's concept of tragedy must be more clearly understood, the real value of the late plays must be more cogently explained, the printing history and influence of Jonson's First Folio must be told--to mention only a few of the tasks future Jonsonian criticism will surely want to undertake. If the past quarter century of criti-

cism is any indication of what is to come, then the last
twenty-five years of the twentieth century promise to be
both productive and exciting ones for Jonsonian scholarship.

NOTES

1. Notable nineteenth-century exceptions include: J. H.
    Penniman, The War of the Theaters (Boston, 1897)
    and R. A. Small, The Stage Quarrel Between Ben
    Jonson and the So-Called Poetasters (Breslau, 1899);
    see also the later historical study of R. G. Noyes,
    Ben Jonson on the English Stage, 1660-1776 (Cam-
    bridge, Mass., 1936).
2. Ben Jonson (New York, 1886), p. 7.
3. See, however, Willa M. Evans' later study, Ben Jon-
    son and Elizabethan Music (Lancaster, Pa., 1929).
4. A Study of Ben Jonson (London, 1889), pp. 114-115.
5. "Ben Jonson and the Classical School," PMLA, 13
    (1898), 221-249; cf. C. F. Wheeler, Classical Myth-
    ology in the Plays, Masques and Poems of Jonson
    (Princeton, 1928) and K. A. McEuen, Classical In-
    fluence Upon the Tribe of Ben (Iowa, 1939).
6. Boston, 1898, p. 15; cf. Eleanor P. Lumley, The In-
    fluence of Plautus on the Comedies of Ben Jonson
    (New York, 1901) and Mina Kerr, The Influence of
    Ben Jonson on English Comedy (Philadelphia, 1912).
7. Paris, 1907, p. 870.
8. Ben Jonson (London, 1919); see also A. C. Howell,
    "A Note on Ben Jonson's Literary Methods," SP, 28
    (Oct. 1931), 710-719; Egerton Clarke, "Ben Jonson's
    Poetry," Dublin Review, 101 (1937), 325-338; L. A.
    Beaurline, "The Selective Principle in Jonson's Short-
    er Poems," Criticism, 8 (1966), 64-74; and the un-
    publ. diss. of Arthur LeRoy Langvordt, "The Verse
    Epigram in England During the Sixteenth and Early
    Seventeenth Centuries," Univ. of Colo., 1956 and
    Ruth Frances Stickney, "Formal Verse Satire From
    Lodge to Jonson, with Particular Reference to the
    Imitation of Classical Models," Univ. of Minn., 1957.
9. "Ben Jonson," Selected Essays (New York, 1965), p. 128.
10. Ibid.
11. "Jonson's Lyric Poetry," Criterion, 13 (1933-34), 430-
    448.
12. Ben Jonson (New York, 1934), p. 300.
13. Drama and Society in the Age of Jonson (New York,
    1937), p. 6.

14. "The Art of Jonson, " E & S, 30 (1944), 49.
15. Ben Jonson: Poet (New York, 1945), p. 47.
16. Ibid., p. 161.
17. The Satiric and the Didactic in Jonson's Comedy (Chapel Hill, 1947), pp. 135, 184; see also the unpubl. diss. of Constantine John Gianakaris, "Humanistic Thought and the Movement of Judgment in Ben Jonson's Comedies, " Univ. of Wisc., 1961.
18. Apologie for Bartholomew Fayre: The Art of Jonson's Comedies (New York, 1947).
19. "Ben Jonson and the Seventeenth Century, " E & S, n. s. 2 (1949), 7-24; cf. Frank B. Fieler, "The Impact of Bacon and the New Science Upon Jonson's Critical Thought in Timber, " Renaissance Papers 1958-60, 84-92.
20. English Literature in the Earlier Seventeenth Century, 1600-1660 (Oxford, 1945), pp. 104-154; see also Bush's English Poetry: The Main Currents from Chaucer to the Present (New York, 1952), pp. 52-55.
21. Literary Criticism: A Short History (New York, 1967), pp. 174-188.
22. "The Rise of English Classicism: A Study in Methodology, " CL, 2 (1950), 267.
23. Religion and Superstition in the Plays of Jonson and Middleton (Upsala, 1950).
24. "The Poet's Morals in Jonson's Poetaster, " MLQ, 12 (1951), 13-19.
25. "The Political Tragedies of Chapman and Ben Jonson, " EIC, 2 (Oct. 1952), 397-412.
26. Ben Jonson of Westminster (New York, 1953).
27. "Ananias the Deacon: A Study of Religion in Jonson's The Alchemist, " English, 9 (1953), 207-212.
28. "Christian Comedy: Volpone, " SP, 51 (1954), 172-193.
29. "Satire and Identification: An Introduction to Ben Jonson, " KR, 19 (Spring 1957), 267-283.
30. Jonson and the Comic Truth (Madison, 1957), p. 207.
31. Ben Jonson (New York, 1959).
32. The Broken Compass: A Study of the Major Comedies of Ben Jonson (London, 1958), p. 63; see also the unpubl. diss. of Forrest Godfrey Read, "Audience, Poet, and Structure in Ben Jonson's Plays, " Cornell, 1962.
33. Ben Jonson and the Language of Prose Comedy (Cambridge, Mass., 1960), pp. 297-298.
34. Ibid., pp. 298-299. For other important discussions of Jonson's language, see Alexander H. Sackton, Rhetoric as a Dramatic Language in Jonson (New

York, 1948); Esko V. Pennanen, Chapters on the Language in Jonson's Dramatic Works (Turku, 1951); A. C. Partridge, The Accidence of Jonson's Plays, Masques, and Entertainments (Cambridge, 1953); A. C. Partridge, Studies in the Syntax of Ben Jonson's Plays (Cambridge, 1953).
35. Ben Jonson's Art: Elizabethan Life and Literature as Reflected Therein (New York, 1963).
36. Ben Jonson: Studies in the Plays (Norman, 1963).
37. Ben Jonson's Plays: An Introduction (Lincoln, 1964).
38. "Bartholomew Fair as Blasphemy," RenD, 8 (1965), 152.
39. The Jonsonian Masque (Cambridge, Mass., 1965); see also the unpubl. diss. of Horton E. Presley, "O Showes, Showes, Mighty Showes: A Study of the Relationship of the Jones-Jonson Controversy to the Rise of Illusionistic Staging in Seventeenth-Century British Drama," Univ. of Kans., 1966.
40. Method and Meaning in Jonson's Masques (Notre Dame, Indiana, 1966).
41. "The Staging of Bartholomew Fair," SEL, 2.2 (1962), 194.
42. "The Themes and Staging of Bartholomew Fair," UTQ, 39 (1970), 306.
43. "Old Comedy in Bartholomew Fair," Criticism, 10 (1968), 290-99.
44. "Ben Jonson: His Aesthetic of Relief," TSLL, 10 (1968), 174.
45. "Ben Jonson and the Illusion of Completeness," PMLA, 84 (1969), 51.
46. "Ben Jonson and the Centered Self," SEL, 10 (1970), 325-48.
47. The Devil's Disciple: Ben Jonson's Debt to Machiavelli (New York, 1969).
48. The Aristophanic Comedies of Ben Jonson (The Hague, 1969), p. 188.
49. Jonson's Moral Comedy (Evanston, 1971), p. 250.
50. Vision and Judgment in Ben Jonson's Drama (New Haven, 1968), pp. 2-3.
51. The Sons of Ben (Detroit, 1967).
52. "The Shaping of Ben Jonson's Career: A Reexamination of Facts and Problems," MP, 67 (1970), 224-37.
53. Ben Jonson's 'Dotages' (Lexington, 1967), p. 8.
54. Ben Jonson's Literary Criticism (Lincoln, 1970).
55. "Sir Epicure Mammon: A Study in Spiritual Fornication," RenQ, 22 (1969), 233-42.
56. "Lovewit's Triumph and Jonsonian Morality: A Read-

ing of The Alchemist, " Criticism, 11 (1969), 166.
57. "Epicoene and the Prose Paradox, " PQ, 49 (1970), 187.
58. "Identifying Ethical Values in Volpone, " HLQ, 32 (1968),
    45-57.
59. "Folly, Incurable Disease, and Volpone, " SEL, 8
    (1968), 348.
60. "Celia, Bonario, and Jonson's Indebtedness to the
    Medieval Cycles, " Etudes Anglaises, 25 (1972), 507.
61. "Jonson's Catiline: History as the Trying Faculty, "
    SP, 67 (1970), 220.
62. Jonson's Romish Plot (Oxford, 1967).
63. "The Self-Reflexive Art of Ben Jonson's Sejanus, "
    TSLL, 12 (1970), 197.
64. "Sejanus and the Ideal Prince Tradition, " SEL, 11
    (1971), 264.
65. "The Tone of Ben Jonson's Poetry, " in Metaphysical to
    Augustan: Studies in Tone and Sensibility in the
    Seventeenth Century (London, 1955), pp. 23-44.
66. "Ben Jonson's Religious Lyrics, " JEGP, 62 (1963), 96-
    110.
67. " 'This So Subtile Sport': Some Aspects of Jonson's
    Epigrams, " Univ. of Colo. Stud., Series in Lang.
    and Lit., 10 (Boulder, 1966), 37-56.
68. "Curse Upon a God: Classical and Elizabethan Thought
    Blended, " Brigham Young Univ. Studies, 5 (1964),
    87-94; see also the unpubl. diss. of Harold Roland
    Swardson, Jr., "A Study of the Tension Between
    Christian and Classical Traditions in Seventeenth-
    Century Poetry, " Univ. of Minn., 1965.
69. "The Christian Wisdom of Ben Jonson's 'On My First
    Sonne, ' " SEL, 11 (1971), 125-136.
70. Ben Jonson's Poems: A Study of the Plain Style (Stan-
    ford, 1962); cf. Arnold Stein's review of Trimpi's
    work, "Plain Style, Plain Criticism, and Ben Jonson,"
    ELH, 30 (1963), 306-316; see also Trimpi's "Jonson
    and the Neo-Latin Authorities for the Plain Style, "
    PMLA, 77 (1962), 21-26.
71. The Poetry of Ben Jonson (New York, 1969).
72. "Pastoral and Counter-Pastoral, " Critical Quarterly,
    10 (1968), 288.
73. "All About Jonson's Poetry, " ELH, 39 (1972), 209.
74. "The Real Toad in the Jonsonian Garden: Resonance
    in the Non-dramatic Poetry, " JEGP, 68 (1969), 5.
75. "Jonson as a Social Realist, " Southern Rev., 6 (1940),
    375-386.
76. "Ben Jonson and the Seventeenth Century" (see note
    19 above), p. 24.

77. See, respectively, notes 17 and 24 above.
78. See note 29 above.
79. See note 25 above and "The Conscience of Politics and
     Jonson's Catiline, " SEL, 6 (1966), 341-356.
80. "The Country House Poem of the Seventeenth Century, "
     JWCI, 19 (1956), 159-174.
81. "On the Growth of a Place and a Poem: Ben Jonson s
     Good Society, " Modern Age, 8 (1963), 64.
82. "A Jonsonian Ideal: 'To Penshurst,' " PQ, 42 (1963),
     14.
83. "Ethical Thought and Ben Jonson's Poetry, " SEL, 9
     (1969), 123-34.
84. "Ben Jonson's 'Chast Booke': The Epigrames, " Renais-
     sance and Modern Studies, 13 (1969), 76-87.
85. "Ben Jonson's Poems: Notes on the Ordered Society, "
     in Essays in English Literature from the Renaissance
     to the Victorian Age (Toronto, 1964), p. 45.

ARTICLES AND NOTES

A1 Allen, Frank. "'Drink to Me Only....'" N&Q, 197
    (1952), 161.
    Favors changing the "objectionable next-to-last
    line." See the reply of J. Burke-Severs, p. 262
    (Item A62 below).

A2 Anderson, Donald K. "The Banquet of Love in English
    Drama (1595-1642)." JEGP, 62 (1964), 422-32.
    A consideration of the "love banquet" of Marston,
    Jonson, Chapman, and others.

A3 Anderson, Mark A. "The Successful Unity of Epicoene:
    A Defense of Ben Jonson." SEL, 10 (1969), 349-
    66.
    "The disguise of Epicoene, symptomatic of the
    deceptions within society, by the deception of both
    the audience and the characters in the play, has in-
    cluded the audience within the society of the play,
    and has shown the real-world society to be equally
    undiscerning, deceivable, and defective" (p. 366).

A4 Anon. "Ben Jonson's Poems." TLS, July 5, 1947.

A5 Arden, John. "An Embarrassment to the Tidy Mind."
    Gambit, 6, No. 22 (1973), 30-46.
    An analysis of Jonson's ideas on dramatic form
    and structure.

A6 Armstrong, William A. "Ben Jonson and Jacobean
    Stagecraft." Jacobean Theatre (Stratford-upon-
    Avon Studies, 1), London: E. Arnold, 1960; New
    York: St. Martin's Press, 1960, pp. 43-61.

A7 Arnold, Judd. "The Double Plot in Volpone: A Note
    on Jonsonian Dramatic Structure." SCN, 23.4
    (1965), 47-8, 50-2.

33

A8   _____. "Lovewit's Triumph and Jonsonian Morality:
         A Reading of The Alchemist. " Criticism, 11 (1969),
         151-166.
              "His [Jonson's] art suggests that he was not com-
         mitted to the general reform of mankind, nor to
         cynically despairing at the impossibility of such re-
         form, but to applauding and enjoying the personal
         triumph of the cavalierly aloof, intellectual aristocrat
         over the hopeless mass of fools. The appreciation
         of such a triumph is logically consistent with Jon-
         son's drawing of a predictable world. If the Great
         Chain of Being necessarily incorporates within it
         that 'variety and throng of humours, ' then Jonson
         as a reformer would by his own dramatically con-
         ceived standards, fall into the category of the zeal-
         ously inspired fool--doubly foolish because he has
         already defined the impossibility of his task. The
         propriety of Lovewit's triumph is consistent with
         Jonson's tolerant but satirically unsentimental por-
         trayal of the world" (p. 166).

A9   Arnstein, Robert. "Volpone and Renaissance Psychol-
         ogy. " N&Q, N. S. 3 (1956), 471-2.

A10   Ashton, Robert. "Usury and High Finance in the Age
         of Shakespeare and Jonson. " Nottingham Renaissance
         and Modern Studies, 4 (1960), 14-43.

A11   Aylward, J. D. "The Inimitable Bobadill. " N&Q, 195
         (1950), 2-4, 28-31.
              Attempts to identify Bobadill (EMI) with Rocco
         Bonetti, an Italian dueling master. Additional de-
         tails about Bonetti are offered in a later note by
         K. T. Butler, N&Q, 195 (1950), 95-97.

A12   _____. "Volpone at Drury Lane. " N&Q, 195 (1950),
         n. pag.

A13   Babb, Howard S. "The 'Epitaph on Elizabeth, L. H. '
         and Ben Jonson's Style. " JEGP, 62 (1963), 738-44.

A14   Babington, Bruce. "Ben Jonson's Poetry of the Sur-
         face. " Words: Wai-Te-Ata Studies in Literature,
         No. 2 (December 1966), p. 66-81.

A15   Bachrach, A. G. H. "Sir Constantyn Huygens and Ben
         Jonson. " Neophilologus, 35 (1951), 120-9.

A16   Bacon, Wallace A.   "The Magnetic Field: The Struc-
      ture of Jonson's Comedies."   HLQ, 19 (1956), 121-
      53.

A17   Bamborough, J. B.   "The Early Life of Ben Jonson."
      TLS, April 8, 1960, p. 225.

A18   _____.   "Joyce and Jonson."   Rev. of Eng. Lit.
      (Leeds), 2.4 (1961), 45-50.

A19   Barish, Jonas A.   "The Double Plot in Volpone."   MP,
      51 (1953), 83-92.
         Reprinted in Ben Jonson: A Collection of Critical
      Essays, ed. Jonas A. Barish.   Englewood Cliffs:
      Prentice-Hall, 1963; see B9.

A20   _____.   "Ovid, Juvenal, and The Silent Woman."
      PMLA, 71 (1956), 213-24.
         Ovid's Ars Amatoriae and Juvenal's Sixth Satire
      are examined as sources for the play.

A21   _____.   "Baroque Prose in the Theatre: Ben Jon-
      son."   PMLA, 73 (1958), 184-95.
         An examination of Jonson's prose style based
      upon the foundations laid by Morris Croll's papers
      on "baroque" 17th century prose, published in the
      1920's, and George Williamson's The Senecan Amble
      (1951).

A22   _____.   "Bartholomew Fair and Its Puppets."   MLQ,
      20 (1959), 3-17.

A23   Barker, J. R.   "A Pendant to Drummond of Haw-
      thornden's Conversations."   RES, 16 (1965), 284-88.

A24   Barnes, Peter, Colin Blakely, Terry Hands, Irving
      Wardle, Jonathan Hammond.   "Ben Jonson and the
      Modern Stage."   Gambit, 6, No. 22 (1973), 5-30.
         A discussion of Jonson's dramatic ability, style,
      appeal, and influence in British theatre.

A25   Barr, C. B. L.   "More Books from Ben Jonson's Li-
      brary."   Book Collector, 13 (1964), 346-48.

A26   Beaurline, L. A.   "The Selective Principle in Jonson's
      Shorter Poems."   Criticism, 8 (1966), 64-74.

A27   _____. "Ben Jonson and the Illusion of Complete-
           ness." PMLA, 84 (1969), 51-59.

A28   Benham, Allen R. "Horace and His Ars Poetica in
           English: A Bibliography." Classical Weekly, 49
           (1956), 1-5.

A29   Bennett, Josephine Waters. "Britain Among the Fortu-
           nate Isles." SP, 53 (1956), 114-140.

A30   _____. "Benson's Alleged Piracy of Shakespeare's
           Sonnetts and of Some of Jonson's Works." SB, 21
           (1968), 235-48.

A31   Bergeron, David M. "Harrison, Jonson and Dekker:
           The Magnificent Entertainment for King James
           (1604)." JWCI, 31 (1968), 445-48.

A32   Bergman, Joseph A. "Shakespeare's 'Purge' of Jon-
           son, Once Again." Emporia State Research Studies,
           15 (1966), 27-33.

A33   Berry, Herbert and E. K. Timings. "Spenser's Pen-
           sion." RES, N.S. 11 (1960), 254-9.
               At one point brings into question the notion of the
           starving poet, promulgated by Jonson.

A34   Bishop, David H. "Shylock's Humour." Shakes.
           Assoc. Bulletin, 23.4 (1948), 174-80.
               Shylock's use of the word (MV, IV.i. 35-62)
           foreshadows Jonson's in EMO.

A35   Blanshard, Rufus A. "Carew and Jonson." SP, 52
           (1955), 195-211.

A36   Blissett, William. "Caesar and Satan." JHI, 18
           (1957), 221-32.
               Concerns "the affinity between Satan and the
           monstrous figure of Caesar which the Elizabethans,
           notably Marlowe and Jonson, inherited from Lucan's
           Pharsalia."

A37   _____. "The Venter Tripartite in The Alchemist."
           SEL, 8 (1968), 323-34.
               The World, the Flesh, and the Devil--the old
           enemies of mankind--constitute the real cheaters in
           the play, disguised as men and women of the time.

Lovewit triumphs in the end as the respectable
worldling.

A38   Blunden, Edmund.   "Shakespeare Oddities."   N&Q,
N.S. 7 (1960), 334-5.
From a footnote in a 19th century song-book:
"Chr. Marlowe was killed by Ben Jonson."

A39   Boas, F. S.   "Edward Howard's Lyrics and Essays."
Contemporary Rev., 174 (1948), 107-11.
Concerning Howard's seventeenth-century tributes
to Shakespeare and Jonson.

A40   Boddy, Margaret.   "A Reading in Jonson's 'Oberon.'"
N&Q, N.S. 18 (Jan. 1971), 29.
On the tradition of Aurora leaving her bed.

A41   [no entry]

A42   Boughner, Daniel C.   "Jonson's Use of Lipsius in Sejanus."   MLN, 73 (1958), 247-55.
Disagrees with Simpson that Jonson used Tacitus
as his source for Sejanus and argues for Lipsius as
the source.

A43   _____.   "'Rhodig' and Sejanus."   N&Q, N.S. 5
(1958), 287-9.
Ludovicus Caelius Richerius Rhodiginus' Anti-
quarium Lectionum Libri XVI, Venice, 1516, was
one of Jonson's sources.

A44   _____.   "Juvenal, Horace, and Sejanus."   MLN, 75
(1960), 545-50.
"To charge Jonson with a rather slavish subser-
vience to Juvenal or Tacitus, it would seem, is to
persevere in blindness to his aims" (p. 550).

A45   _____.   "Sejanus and Machiavelli."   SEL, 1.2
(1961), 81-100.
The Florentine secretary had already studied a
problem in suspense that did not exist in Roman
history: whether such a prince as Tiberius might,
by such 'artes,' trick such a formidable antagonist
as Sejanus into a fatal confidence.   Jonson develops
this germ of drama by a series of climactic actions
based on the devious skill in politics expounded in
The Prince.   For the reversal at the end of his

play, he returns to Machiavelli's solution of the problem illustrated by the same adversaries in The Discourses on Livy, itself a reinterpretation of Tacitus's Annals. " (See especially pp. 81-82.)

A46   . "Lewkenor and 'Volpone.' " N&Q, N. S. 9 (1962), 124-30.
        Examines Jonson's use of Lewis Lewkenor's The Commonwealth & Government of Venice (1599).

A47   . "Jonsonian Structure in The Tempest. " SQ, 21 (1970), 3-10.
        Structural elements in EMI and Temp. deriving from Aelius Donatus (prologue, protasis, epitasis, and catastrophe) evaluated against the perhaps "irrelevant" convention of the 5-act division.

A48   Boyd, John D. "T. S. Eliot As Critic and Rhetorician: The Essay on Jonson. " Criticism, 11 (1969), 167-182.

A49   Bradbrook, F. W. "John Donne and Ben Jonson. " N&Q, N. S. 4 (1957), 146-7.
        The opening of Volpone may echo "The Sunne Rising. "

A50   Bredvold, Louis I. "The Rise of English Classicism: A Study in Methodology. " CL, 3 (1950), 253-68.
        "The comparatist studying French influence must always take account of the enormous prestige of Jonson as the founder of classicism in English drama and poetry" (p. 255).

A51   Brooks, Harold F. "A Satyricall Shrub. " TLS, Dec. 11, 1969, p. 1426.
        "Rodomontade, " attributed to Rochester, is taken largely from Jonson.

A52   Brown, A. D. Fitton. "Drink to Me, Celia. " MLR, 54 (1959), 554-7.
        Jonson's debt to the Greek original of the Epistles of Philostratus and to its Latin translations by Antonio Bonfini in Epistolae Graeconicae (Geneva, 1606).

A53   Brown, Arthur. "Citizen Comedy and Domestic Drama. " Jacobean Theatre (Stratford-upon-Avon Studies, 1), New York: St. Martins Press, 1960;

London: E. Arnold, 1960, pp. 63-83.

A54   Brown, Ivor. "Not So Big Ben." Drama (Winter
       1970), pp. 44-46.
       Jonson's reputation is countered to Shakespeare's.

A55   Bryant, Joseph A., Jr. "The Nature of the Conflict
       in Jonson's Sejanus." Vanderbilt Stud. in the Hu-
       manities, 1 (1951), 197-219.
       The "conflict" is between good and evil, not be-
       tween Sejanus and Tiberius.

A56   _____. "The Significance of Ben Jonson's First Re-
       quirement for Tragedy: 'Truth of Argument.'" SP,
       49 (1952), 195-213.
       To Jonson "truth of argument" implied an histori-
       cal argument capable of being presented with veri-
       similitude. Jonson transferred the traditional aim
       of history (expressed in Underwood, XXIV) to trage-
       dy. "Jonson's tragedies ... though written to edify
       the masses, are written so far above the knowledge
       that anyone but Jonson would have expected of the
       masses that only the specially learned can compre-
       hend them at first reading" (p. 212).

A57   _____. "Catiline and the Nature of Jonson's Tragic
       Fable." PMLA, 69 (1954), 265-77.
       "It can be shown, I think, that Jonson's ordering
       of his fable, rightly understood, gives the clue to
       why and how he expected these plays to be judged
       as tragedies rather than merely as serious history
       plays. In other words, it lets one see the concep-
       tion of tragic drama that he worked by" (p. 265).

A58   _____. "Jonson's Revision of Every Man in His
       Humor." SP, 59 (1962), 641-50.
       Discusses Jonson's adaptation of Roman comic in-
       trigue. EMI shows a fascination with humour theory
       only as a means of characterization. Before he re-
       published EMI, Jonson cut away the superfluous
       moralizing about poetry and reshaped it in terms of
       humours.

A59   _____. "Jonson's Satirist Out of his Humor." Ball
       State Teachers College Forum, 3.1 (1962), 31-6.
       "Confident as he was of the power of his art and
       the loyalty of his muses, Jonson had come to recog-

nize that no amount of private morality or artistic
skill could compensate for one lack which somewhat
earlier had seemed destined to preclude his achieving that office of public satarist for which he felt
nature had intended him" (p. 31).

A60 [no entry]

A61 Bullett, Gerald. "'Drink to Me Only....'" TLS,
     June 1, 1956, p. 329.
        Would emend for to fro (= from) in "I would not
     change for thine." But E. A. Horsman, June 8,
     1956, p. 345, notes that change means exchange;
     see also letter by Daniel George, June 8, p. 345.

A62 Burke-Severs, J. "'Drink to Me Only....'" N&Q,
     197 (1952), 262.
        In answer to Frank Allen (see A1) argues against
     changing the "objectionable" next-to-last line.

A63 Burton, K. M. "The Political Tragedies of Chapman
     and Ben Jonson." EIC, 2 (1952), 397-412.
        "Chapman and Jonson are concerned with the
     tragic flaw within the social order, not within the
     individual. Although they differ as to the immediate
     causes of the corruption which flaws the social struc-
     ture, each presents a dilemma in which society as
     a whole is involved" (p. 397).

A64 Buxton, John. "The Poet's Hall Called Apollo." MLR,
     48 (1953), 52-54.
        Drayton's The Sacrifice to Apollo, Jonson's
     Leges Convivales, and the Devil Tavern.

A65 Cable, Chester A. "Oldham's Borrowing from Buchan-
     an." MLN, 66 (1951), 523-7.
        While admitting that Jonson's Catiline is Oldham's
     chief source for his Satyrs upon the Jesuits, argues
     that "Loyda's Will" is based upon George Buchanan's
     Franciscanus.

A66 Calder, Daniel G. "The Meaning of 'Imitation' in Jon-
     son's Discoveries." NM, 70 (1969), 435-40.

A67 Caldiero, Frank. "Ben Jonson's Course in Freshman
     English." CE, 19 (1957), 7-11.

A68   Camden, Carroll. "Spenser's 'Little Fish That Men
      Call Remora.'" <u>Rice Inst. Pamphlet</u>, 44.1 (1957),
      1-12.
          Diverse accounts of the <u>remora</u> or <u>echeneis</u> in
      Jonson and others.

A69   Cannon, Charles K. "The Relation of the Additions of
      <u>The Spanish Tragedy</u> to the Original Play." <u>SEL</u>,
      2.2 (1962), 229-39.

A70   Carpenter, Charles A. "<u>Epicoene</u> Minus Its Secret:
      Surprise As Expectation." <u>Xavier University Studies</u>,
      7.3 (1968), 15-22.

A71   Champion, L. S. "The Comic Intent of Jonson's <u>The
      New Inn.</u>" <u>Western Humanities Rev.</u>, 18 (1964),
      66-74.

A72   _____. "<u>The Magnetic Lady</u>: The Close of Ben
      Jonson's Circle." <u>Southern Humanities Rev.</u>, 2
      (1968), 104-21.

A73   Chan, Mary. "<u>Cynthia's Revels</u> and Music for a Choir
      School: Christ Church Manuscript Mus 439." <u>SR</u>,
      18 (1971), 134-172.
          "A study of the manuscript together with a con-
      sideration of the function of Hedon's song in <u>Cynthia's
      Revels</u> is particularly illuminating: for in Hedon
      Jonson appears to be parodying characteristics of
      much of the music in the 439 manuscript. While
      our conclusions are valuable only in so far as they
      are accepted as hypothetical, nevertheless the
      Christ Church manuscript seems on close study to
      have a homogeneity in its contents and characteris-
      tics which may very well be more than purely acci-
      dental" (pp. 134-35).

A74   Clancy, James H. "Ben Jonson and the 'Humours.'"
      <u>Theatre Annual</u>, 11 (1953), 15-23.

A75   Clary, Frank N., Jr. "The Vol and the Pone: A Re-
      consideration of Jonson's <u>Volpone.</u>" <u>ELN</u>, 10 (Dec.
      1972), 102-107.
          "Vol" in the language of heraldry and falconry
      is "a Lure, in Blazon"; a "pone" in legal termi-
      nology is "a writ requiring the sheriff to secure
      the appearance of the defendant by attaching his

goods or by causing him to find sureties for his
appearance. " The essay concludes, "the specialized
definitions of the terms vol and pone provide the
keys to Jonson's wit at the end of Volpone; the "jar-
gons" of heraldry, falconry, and law combine with
conventionally accepted beast fable to lend additional
dimension to Jonson's play about fraud, for the
double title is itself fraudulent" (p. 107).

A76   Clausen, Wendell. "The Beginnings of English Charac-
        ter Writing in the Early Seventeenth Century. " PQ,
        25 (1946), 32-45.

A77   Cloudsley, Annabella. "Volpone in Germany. " Twenti-
        eth Century, 168 (1960), 66-9.
            On the première of Francis Burt's operatic adap-
        tation.

A78   Clubb, Roger L. "The Paradox of Ben Jonson's 'A
        Fit of Rime Against Rime.'" College Lang. Assoc.
        Journal (Morgan State College, Baltimore), 5 (1961),
        145-7.

A79   Coiseault-Cavalca, M. "Les Romantiques français et
        les Elisabethains. " Les Lettres Romanes (Louvain),
        20 (1966), 334-55.
            Study of the French translation of certain plays
        by Marlowe and by Jonson, considering the picture
        of Elizabethan society given by French critics of
        the period.

A80   Combellack, Frederick M. "Jonson's 'To John Donne.'"
        Expl., 17 (1958), No. 1, Item 6.
            Gives prose translation of Jonson's poem.

A81   Cookman, A. V. "Shakespeare's Contemporaries on
        the Modern English Stage. " SJ 94 (1958), 29-41.
            Marlowe, Jonson, and others.

A82   Cope, Jackson I. "Volpone and the Authorship of
        Eastward Hoe. " MLN, 72 (1957), 253-6.
            On the basis of the similarity of Securitie's self-
        defense (EH. II. ii. 94-124) to Volpone's opening dia-
        logue with Mosca, argues that Jonson "wrote the
        passage in Eastward Hoe rather than adapting from
        one of his collaborators. "

A83 _____ . "Jonson on the Christ's College Dons."
MLN, 74 (1959), 101-2.
The Magnetick Lady, I.v.10-20, alludes to three
rival parties at Christ's College, Cambridge. Jonson, who may have learned of the college's religious
politics from Nathaniel Tovey, perhaps wrote the
episode into his play for the benefit of his specta-
tors familiar with Cambridge quarrels.

A84 _____ . "Jonson's Reading of Spenser: The Genesis
of a Poem." EM, 10 (1959), 61-6.
Jonson's "Epistle to Elizabeth Countess of Rut-
land" (The Forest, XII) derives from Spenser's
Mother Hubbard's Tale, ii.152-154, and other
Spenser poems.

A85 _____ . "The Date of Middleton's Women Beware
Women." MLN, 76 (1961), 295-300.
Believes the play was written 1613-14, probably
shortly after Middleton's The Triumphs of Truth,
which shows the influence of Jonson's Hymenaei.

A86 _____ . "Bartholomew Fair as Blasphemy." RenD,
8 (1965), 127-52.

A87 Cox, Gerald H., III. "Celia, Bonario, and Jonson's
Indebtedness to the Medieval Cycles." Etudes Anglaises, 25 (1972), 506-11.
"Jonson's treatment of Celia, and to a lesser
degree, Bonario, is remarkably similar to that of
the sacred figures in the Corpus Christi plays.
First, like Christ or the Virgin, Celia is placed
in the midst of natural or unredeemed men, but such
is her virtue that she withstands temptation and remains uncorrupted. Second, like these holy figures,
Celia and Bonario say relatively little--their pre-
sence is almost more important than their words"
(p. 507).

A88 Craik, T. W. "Volpone's 'Young Antinous.'" N&Q,
17 (1970), 213-14.

A89 Cross, Gustav. "The Authorship of Lust's Dominion."
SP, 55 (1958), 39-61.
Believes Marston authored parts, pointing to
"neologisms and Marstonian coinages," and points
out that a number of these were satirized by Jon-

son in <u>Poetaster</u>, where he had Marston in mind in
the character of Crispinus.

A90   Cubeta, Paul M. "'A Celebration of Charis': An
      Evaluation of Jonsonian Poetic Strategy. " <u>ELH</u>, 25
      (1958), 163-80.
      "Because of his remarkable feat in combining the
      mode of much Greek and Latin love poetry with the
      manner of Spenser, Donne, and Pope, this poem
      holds a pivotal position halfway between the tradi-
      tions of the sixteenth and eighteenth centuries" (p.
      163).

A91   _____. "Ben Jonson's Religious Lyrics. " <u>JEGP</u>,
      62 (1963), 96-110.
      Discusses the influence on Jonson's religious
      verse of the medieval or Renaissance meditative
      exercises of St. Bernard of Clairvaux and St. Ig-
      natius Loyola. This tradition links Jonson's devo-
      tional poetry to that of Robert Southwell, John
      Donne, and George Herbert.

A92   _____. "A Jonsonian Ideal: 'To Penshurst.' " <u>PQ</u>,
      42 (1963), 14-24.
      "Jonson's technique for defining his personal and
      social ethics is to establish the ideal, whether it
      be a moral value, a noble character, or a Utopian
      world, in sharp contrast with the empirical reality
      of the world he lives in" (p. 14).

A93   Cunningham, Dolora. "The Jonsonian Masque as a
      Literary Form. " <u>ELH</u>, 22 (1955), 108-24.

A94   Currey, R. N. "Jonson and <u>The Tempest</u>. " <u>N&Q</u>,
      192 (1947), 468.
      Reports a lecture by R. C. Howarth.

A95   Cutts, John P. "British Museum Add. MS. 31432
      William Lawes' Writing for the Theatre and the
      Court. " <u>The Library</u>, Series 5, 7 (1952), 225-34.
      Identifies nine songs, one from Jonson's <u>Enter-
      tainment at Welbeck</u>.

A96   _____. "Jacobean Masque and Stage Music. " <u>Mu-
      sic and Letters</u>, 35 (1954), 185-200.

A97   _____. "Original Music to Browne's Inner Temple

Masque, and Other Jacobean Masque Music."
N&Q, N.S. 1 (1954), 194-5.
Reports discovery of new musical settings by
Robert Johnson and Alphonso Ferrabosco of songs
from William Browne's Masque, Daniel's Hymen's
Triumph (as well as of Daniel's Sonnet VI), Jon-
son's Oberon, and Campion's Lord's Masque.

A98   . "Ben Jonson's Masque 'The Vision of De-
       light.'" N&Q, N.S. 3 (1956), 64-7.
       Transcribes a contemporary musical setting of
       the epilogue to Jonson's Masque, after indicating
       its significance for the history of song in seven-
       teenth-century English masques.

A99   . "Le Rôle de la Musique dans les Masques
       de Ben Jonson et Notamment dans Oberon (1610-
       1611)". Fêtes de la Renaissance (1957), pp. 285-
       303.

A100   . "Volpone's Song: A Note on the Source
       and Jonson's Translation." N&Q, N.S. 5 (1958),
       217-9.

A101   . "Robert Johnson and the Court Masque."
       Music and Letters, 41 (1960), 111-126.
       Composer of music to Jonson's masques.

A102   . "'When Were the Senses in Such Order
       Plac'd?'" CompD, 4 (1970), 52-62.
       Discussion of Love's Welcome at Bolsover.

A103   . "Seventeenth-Century Illustrations of
       Three Masques by Jonson." CompD, 6 (Summer
       1972), 125-134.
       "Students of Jonson's masques interested in
       their visual aspect have always depended very
       heavily on Jonson's own occasionally detailed des-
       criptions of their scenes and choreography ... and
       particularly of recent years on Inigo Jones' archi-
       tectural and costume designs but it has not hither-
       to been noticed that illustrations for at least three
       of his masques, The Gypsies Metamorphosed,
       Augures, and For the Honour of Wales, were
       available in print and together not many years
       after the masques were produced" (p. 125).

A104   D., A.   "The Genesis of Jonson's Epicoene."   N&Q,
        193 (1948), 55-6.
        Jonson may have developed Epicoene from Wil-
        liam Rankin's Satyrus Peregrinans.

A105   Dale, Leona.   "Jonson's Sick-Society."   BRMMLA,
        24 (1970), 66-74.

A106   Danby, John F.   "The Poets on Fortune's Hill: Lit-
        erature and Society, 1580-1610."   Cambridge Jour.,
        2 (1949), 195-211.
        Emphasis placed upon Sidney, Spenser, Donne,
        Jonson.

A107   Davis, Tom.   "Ben Jonson's Ode to Himself: An
        Early Version."   PQ, 5 (1972), 410-21.

A108   Davison, Peter H.   "Volpone and the Old Comedy."
        MLQ, 24 (1963), 151-7.
        "Though Jonson adapts what he takes from the
        Old Comedy and is more concerned with serious
        issues, one can see how essential the Old Comedy
        relationship of Impostor and Ironical Buffoon is to
        the play: it is this relationship that makes clear
        the nature of the drama of Volpone" (p. 157).

A109   Dessen, Alan C.   "The Alchemist: Jonson's 'Estates'
        Play."   RenD, 7 (1964), 35-54.
        "The Alchemist is not a morality play, nor are
        its antecedents to be found solely in the English
        allegorical drama.   Jonson, however, has trans-
        formed the traditional conflict between Vice or set
        of Vices and a group of representative 'estates'
        into a 'literal' conflict between a group of business-
        like rogues and a panoramic cross section of
        figures from English society" (p. 49).

A110   _____.   "Volpone and the Late Morality Tradi-
        tion."   MLQ, 25 (1964), 383-99.

A111   _____.   "Jonson's 'Knave of Clubs' and 'The Play
        of the Cards.'"   MLR, 62 (1967), 584-5.

A112   DeVilliers, Jacob I.   "Ben Jonson's Tragedies."   ES,
        45 (1964), 433-42.

A113   Dircks, Richard J.   "Garrick and Gentleman: Two

Interpretations of Abel Drugger." Restoration and
18th Century Theatre Research, 7. 2 (1968), 48-55.

A114   Donaldson, Ian. "'A Martyr's Resolution': Jonson's
Epicoene." RES, N. S. 18(1967), 1-15.
        Building on C. L. Barber's ideas (Shakespeare's
Festive Comedies), Donaldson believes "that unity
of Epicoene may become more apparent if the play
is seen not primarily in relation to New Comedy
or to Old, but rather to a kind of native drama
which has been called 'festive'" (p. 3).

A115   _____. "Jonson's Tortoise." RES, N. S. 19
(1968), 162-66.
        On the significance of the tortoise shell in Vol-
pone.

A116   _____. "Volpone--Quick and Dead." EIC, 21
(1971), 121-134.
        "Jonson's striking and unusual achievement in
Volpone is his placing of the agreeably amoral ac-
tivities of Mosca and Volpone within this chillingly
long perspective of time. Few comedies suggest
so powerfully the yielding of the forces of 'quick-
ness' to the fact of death" (p. 134).

A117   _____. "Damned by Analogies: OR, How to Get
Rid of Ben Jonson." Gambit, 6, No. 22 (1973),
38-46.
        An analysis of the implications of the metaphors
used by a number of critics who have damned Jonson as a dramatist.

A118   Dorenkamp, Angela G. "Jonson's Catiline: History
as the Trying Faculty." SP, 67 (1970), 210-20.
        If history is the shaping spirit of Jonson's art
in Catiline, if, for him, 'the tragic muse is really
the muse of history, and the tragic poet becomes
the poet of history,' then he should not be tried in
the court of Aristotle, or Seneca, or Horace, or
Shakespeare. What he has achieved, certainly, is
not 'an extension rather than a restriction of the
scope of tragedy,' as Bryant says, but an extension of the scope of history. It is the people,
after all, the Chorus, who lack the historical perspective. It is to Jonson's credit that he does
not attempt to cheat them, and that the purity of

his matter remains for the most part unadulterated
by the exigencies of the drama" (p. 220).

A119   Doughtie, Edward. "Ferrabosco and Jonson's 'The
       Houreglasse.'"   RenQ, 22 (1969), 148-150.
       Ferrabosco's music to another song was origi-
       nally intended for Jonson's poem.

A120   Douglass, James W.   "'To Penshurst.'"   Christian
       Scholar, 44 (1961), 133-8.

A121   Draper, R. P.   "The Golden Age and Volpone's Ad-
       dress to his Gold."   N&Q, N. S. 3 (1956), 191-2.
       "[In I. i. 30-40] it is the measure of Volpone's
       audacity and perversity that he can distort the
       Ovidean account of the Golden Age to glorify his
       own 'cunning purchase' of his wealth."

A122   Duffy, Ellen M. T.   "Ben Jonson's Debt to Renais-
       sance Scholarship in 'Sejanus' and 'Catiline.'"
       MLR, 42 (1947), 24-30.
       This essay attempts "to show that in Catiline
       Jonson made extensive use of Durantinus's His-
       toria; that for Sejanus he had recourse to the work
       of Lipsius, and to the commentaries of the Basel
       edition of Sallust for Catiline" (p. 24).

A123   Duncan, Douglas.   "Ben Jonson's Lucianic Irony."
       ArielE, 1. 2 (1970), 42-53.

A124   _____. "A Guide to The New Inn."   EIC, 20
       (1970), 311-26.
       The New Inn is a spoof of romantic comedy, in-
       tentionally ironic in its ridiculousness.

A125   Duncan, Edgar Hill.   "Jonson's Alchemist and the
       Literature of Alchemy."   PMLA, 41 (1946), 699-
       710.
       "When Jonson turned to alchemy as a subject
       for his satiric pen (and it should be remembered
       that alchemy is far from being the only suspect ac-
       tivity he holds up to ridicule in this play), he did
       not find it necessary to exaggerate or distort the
       claims made for the 'science' in alchemical litera-
       ture, as he did, for instance, in the case of the
       Puritan religion.   Here was material ready to his
       hand of the right admixture of pretentious learning

and bizarre humbug perfectly suited to his comic
genius" (p. 710).

A126   Dunlap, Rhodes. "The Allegorical Interpretation of
Renaissance Literature." PMLA, 82 (1967), 39-43.
Draws examples from Jonson, Shakespeare,
Spenser, Tasso, and others.

A127   Echeruo, Michael J. C. "The Conscience of Politics
and Jonson's Catiline." SEL, 6 (1966), 341-56.
"The play is concerned with a historical and a
political process, and accordingly, not only the
conspiracy (which is the occasion for the play),
but also the means of thwarting that conspiracy
become necessary subjects for study" (p. 347).

A128   Ekeblad, Inga-Stina. "A Note on Ben Jonson's
Hymenaei (ii. 56-58 and 182-185)." N&Q, N.S. 3
(1956), 510-11.

A129   Elton, William. "Shakespeare's Portrait of Ajax in
Troilus and Cressida." PMLA, 63 (1948), 744-8.
Conjecturally identifies Ajax as a portrait of
Jonson.

A130   Empson, William. "Volpone." HudR, 21 (1968), 651-
66.
Argues that one should take a more "jovial" at-
titude toward the play.

A131   Emslie, MacDonald. "Three Early Settings of Jon-
son." N&Q, 198 (1953), 466-8.
Adds to the list of musical settings of songs in
Herford and Simpson, XI, 605-9.

A132   _____ . "Nicholas Lanier's Innovations in English
Song." Music and Letters, 41 (1960), 13-32.

A133   Enck, John Jacob. "The Case Is Altered: Initial
Comedy of Humours." SP, 50 (1953), 195-214.

A134   _____ . "The Peace of the Poetomachia." PMLA,
77 (1962), 386-96.
Points up the influence of Jonson upon the tone,
characters, plot, and structure of Troilus and
Cressida.

A135   Enright, D. J.   "Crime and Punishment in Ben Jon-
       son. "   Scrutiny, 9 (1940), 231-48.
            "This theme, what Jonson is concerned with in
       his drama, is what we may call 'spiritual modesty,'
       or the acknowledgement by the individual of his
       proper and ordained position in the universe.   All
       the plays are 'satire' in that they deal with per-
       sons from whom this acknowledgement, this modes-
       ty, is absent, and with the ambitions of these per-
       sons to exist in Brave New Worlds of some or
       other kind of Splendour, with their crime and their
       punishment.   There is always this essential scheme
       of crime and punishment, and the crime is invari-
       ably of the same kind, though its gravity and the
       gravity of the punishment are hardly the same in
       any two plays.   Jonson repeated his lesson without
       repeating himself" (p. 231).

A136   _____ .   "Poetic Satire and Satire in Verse: A
       Consideration of Ben Jonson and Phillip Massinger."
       Scrutiny, 18 (1952), 211-23.

A137   Evans, K. W.   "Sejanus and the Ideal Prince Tradi-
       tion. "   SEL, 11 (1971), 249-264.
            "Sejanus is a brilliant satire on the struggle for
       power and the trends towards despotism in Jaco-
       bean England, constantly shifting in tone from the
       macabre comedy played out by Sejanus and Tiberi-
       us to the misery of Rome's civic tragedy" (p. 264).

A138   Everett, Barbara.   "Ben Jonson's 'A Vision of
       Beauty.' "   Critical Quar., 1 (1959), 238-44.
       A lyric from The New Inn.

A139   Fabian, B.   "'Cynthia' in the O. E. D. "   N&Q, N. S.
       6 (1959), 356.
            Two occurrences of the word, in Marlowe and
       Jonson, antedate the first O. E. D. citation from Il
       Penseroso.

A140   Farmer, Norman K., Jr.   "A Theory of Genre for
       Seventeenth-Century Poetry. "   Genre, 3 (1970),
       293-317.
            Includes discussion of Jonson.

A141   Feather, John.   "Some Notes on the Setting of Quarto
       Plays. "   The Library, 5th Ser., 27:3 (Sept. 1972),

237-244.

One example--"a special, possibly unique in-
stance"--of setting outside the measure is noted
from the works of Jonson: "It occurs on B4 of
The Alchemist, where two words of the text in
line 6 are set outside the measure.... This short
speech does not seem to have been added in proof,
as might be thought; there are press variants known
in this forme, but neither Herford and Simpson nor
F. H. Mares record such a variant here. It is
possible that at some earlier stage of the proofing
than that represented by the extant variants an
omission was discovered, and repaired by the in-
sertion of the additional words" (p. 244).

A142   Feldman, Abraham B. "Playwrights and Pike-
        Trailers in the Low Countries." N&Q, 198 (1953),
        184-7.
        Comments on Gascoigne, William Kempe, Mar-
        lowe, and Jonson.

A143   Fellowes, Peter. "Jonson's Epigrams, CIII (To
        Mary Lady Wroth)." Expl., 31 (Jan. 1973), 36.

A144   Ferns, John. "Ovid, Juvenal, and The Silent Woman:
        A Reconsideration." MLR, 65 (1970), 248-53.

A145   Fike, Francis. "Ben Jonson's 'On My First Sonne.'"
        GorR, 11 (1969), 205-20.

A146   Fisher, William N. "Occupatio in Sixteenth- and
        Seventeenth-Century Verse." TSLL, 19.2 (1972),
        203-222.
        See the discussion of Jonson ("whose use of
        simple occupatio is so skilled and economical that
        careful reading is imperative") that begins on
        p. 213.

A147   [no entry]

A148   Fox, Robert C. "A Source for Milton's Comus."
        N&Q, 9 (1962), 52-3.
        In Poetaster, III.iv.114-116.

A149   Frajnd, Marta. "Teorijski stavovi Bena Džonsona
        [Theoretical Viewpoints of Ben Jonson]." Filoloski
        Pregled (Belgrade), 1-2 (1964), 231-45.

A150   Freehafer, John. "Leonard Digges, Ben Jonson, and
        The Beginning of Shakespeare Idolatry." SQ, 21
        (1970), 63-75.
            Suggests that Digges' poem commending Shakes-
        peare, presumably written for The Second Folio,
        was excluded because of venomous references to
        Ben Jonson.

A151   Freeman, Arthur. "The Earliest Allusion to Volpone."
        N&Q, 14 (1967), 207-8.

A152   French, John T. "Ben Jonson: His Aesthetic of Re-
        lief." TSLL, 10 (1968), 161-75.
            "I speak here, of course, of Jonson's appropria-
        tion of the ancient Greek concept of physical purga-
        tion as a form of relief (literal and figurative) for
        the passions ... " (p. 163). "If this view of purgation
        as an aesthetic formula which satisfies physical
        and epistemological demands be accepted, we may
        conclude that Jonson did have something like a
        philosophical development which he refused to push
        beyond the humanistic formula of his concept of
        art" (p. 174).

A153   Fried, Gisela. "Das Charakterbild Shakespeares im
        17. und 18. Jahrhundert." Jahrbuch der Deutschen
        Shakespeare-Gesellschaft-West, 1965, pp. 161-183.
            Early appraisals of Shakespeare from the writ-
        ings of Jonson, Dryden, and others.

A154   Frost, David. "Shakespeare in the Seventeenth Cen-
        tury." SQ, 16 (1965), 81-89.
            Takes issue with G. E. Bentley's thesis (Shake-
        speare and Jonson, 1945) that Jonson was the
        more highly esteemed poet in the 17th century.

A155   Furniss, W. Todd. "The Annotation of Ben Jonson's
        Masque of Queenes." RES, 5 (1954), 344-60.
            Provides a list of works Jonson used in making
        his notes, as well as a commentary on the anno-
        tations.

A156   _____. "Jonson, Camden, and the Black Prince's
        Plumes." MLN, 69 (1954), 487-8.
            Camden is the source for a detail in Prince
        Henries Barriers.

A157 _____. "Jonson's Antimasques." RN, 7 (1954),
            21-2.

A158 Gerritsen, Johan. "Stansby and Jonson Produce A
      Folio: A Preliminary Account." ES, 40 (1959),
      52-5.

A159 Gianakaris, C. J. "Identifying Ethical Values in Vol-
      pone." HLQ, 32 (1968), 45-57.
            "Sound, reasonable conduct turns out to be the
      sum of the values within Volpone. Accordingly,
      mental powers become the positive attribute rather
      than any ethically oriented goodness. Jonson
      recognized that his audiences would bring conven-
      tional morals to the theatre and would therefore
      not accept Volpone's attempted attack on Celia as
      laudable behavior. For this reason Jonson did
      not seek to underline our traditional morality;
      harking back to a broader humanistic foundation,
      he placed less emphasis on the lack of purely
      ethical scruples than he did on deviation from
      common sense. When good reason is violated by
      one of his characters, Jonson is prompt in bring-
      ing to bear his instrument of ridicule, the comic
      manager within a play. It is Jonson's intention
      that our sympathy in his comedies lie with the
      alert mind instead of the dullard" (pp. 56-57).

A160 Gibson, C. A. "Massinger's Use of His Sources for
      the Roman Actor." Journal of Australasian Uni-
      versities Language Assoc., No. 15 (May 1961),
      61-72.
            Lists Jonson's Sejanus among Massinger's Eng-
      lish sources.

A161 Gilbert, Allan H. "The Italian Names In Every Man
      Out of His Humour." SP, 44 (1947), 195-208.
            The intention of the characters is elucidated by
      the definitions in Florio's A Worlde of Wordes.

A162 _____. "Jonson and Drummond or Gil on the
      King's Senses." MLN, 62 (1947), 35-7.
            On the poem For the Kinge, doubtfully attributed
      to Drummond.

A163 _____. "The Eavesdroppers in Jonson's Sejanus."
      MLN, 69 (1954), 164-6.

A164   Goldberg, S. L. "Folly into Crime: The Catastro-
        phe of Volpone." MLQ, 20 (1959), 233-42.
        "All the moral perversions in the play, from
        Volpone's sensual naturalism to the miserable
        avarice of the suitors, from the brilliant Machia-
        vellianism of Mosca to its farcical parody in Sir
        Politic, from Scoto's quackery to Corvino's jeal-
        ousy, are the outcome and the dramatic expression
        of fundamental delusion" (p. 234).

A165   Goldsmith, Robert H. "The Wild Man on the English
        Stage." MLR, 53 (1958), 481-491.
        The "wild man" as dramatic type, from his
        earliest appearances in sword dances and mum-
        mings to Caliban and Jonson's Silvanes (in the
        Masque of Oberon, 1611).

A166   Gombosi, Otto. "Some Musical Aspects of the Eng-
        lish Court Masque." Journal of the American
        Musicological Society, 1 (1948), 3-19.

A167   Gordon, D. J. "Hymenaei: Ben Jonson's Masque of
        Union." JWCI, 8 (1945), 107-145.

A168   _____. "Ben Jonson's 'Haddington Masque': The
        Story and the Fable." MLR, 42 (1947), 180-7.
        Jonson borrowed from contemporary scholarship
        for his details, but transformed "the story into a
        fable ... about marriage."

A169   _____. "Poet and Architect: The Intellectual Set-
        ting of the Quarrel Between Ben Jonson and Inigo
        Jones." JWCI, 12 (1949), 152-178.

A170   Gossett, Suzanne. "Masque Influence on the Drama-
        turgy of Beaumont and Fletcher." MP, 69 (1972),
        199-208.
        Several Jonsonian masques are discussed in her
        attempt to demonstrate this influence.

A171   Gottwald, Maria. "Ben Jonson's Theory of Comedy."
        Germanica Wratislaviensia (Wroclaw), 10 (1966),
        31-53.

A172   _____. "Koncepcja 'Humorów' u Beniamina John-
        sona." Germanica Wratislaviensia (Wroclaw), 12
        (1968), 3-14.

A173   Gray, Henry David.   "The Chamberlain's Men and the
       'Poetaster.'"   MLR, 42 (1947), 173-9.
              Offers identification of characters in the play,
       and argues that Aesop was intended as an attack
       on Shakespeare for supposedly preventing the per-
       formance of Cynthia's Revels at court.

A174   _____, H. David and Percy Simpson.   "Shake-
       speare or Heminge?   A Rejoinder and a Surre-
       joinder." [Surrejoinder by Simpson, p. 151-2].
       MLR, 45 (1950), 148-152.
              Concerns the identification of Aesop in Poetaster.

A175   Graziani, R. I. C.   "Ben Jonson's Chloridia: Fame
       and her Attendants."   RES, 7 (1956), 56-8.
              Poesy and History represent the contributions
       of Jonson to Fame (or the art of the masque);
       Architecture and Sculpture, those of Inigo Jones.
       Sculpture was added to the other three attendants
       to assist them in literally holding up Lady Fame.

A176   Greene, Thomas M.   "Ben Jonson e l'io accentrato."
       SCr, 3 (1969), 236-62.

A177   _____.   "Ben Jonson and the Centered Self."   SEL,
       10 (1970), 325-48.
              "In Jonson, the associations of the circle as
       metaphysical, political, and moral ideal, as pro-
       portion and equilibrium, as cosmos, realm, so-
       ciety, estate, marriage, harmonious soul--are
       doubled by the associations of a center--governor,
       participant, house, inner self, identity, or when
       the outer circle is broken, as lonely critic and
       self-reliant solitary.   Center and circle become
       symbols, not only of harmony and completeness
       but of stability, repose, fixation, duration, and
       the incompleted circle, uncentered and misshapen,
       comes to symbolize a flux or a mobility, gro-
       tesquely or dazzlingly fluid.   Most of the works in
       Jonson's large canon--including the tragedies and
       comedies, verse and prose--can be categorized
       broadly in their relation to an implicit or explicit
       center" (p. 326).

A178   Greg, W. W.   "Shakespeare and Jonson."   RES, 22
       (1946), 58.
              "Writers might praise and quote Jonson; it was

Shakespeare that people read. "

A179   Gunby, D. C. "Webster: Another Borrowing from
        Jonson's Sejanus. " N&Q, 17 (1970), 214.

A180   H., I. "The Alchemist. " Manchester Guardian Week-
        ly. Jan. 23, 1947, p. 9.

A181   Halio, Jay L. "The Metaphor of Conception and
        Elizabethan Theories of the Imagination. " Neo-
        philologus, 50 (1966), 454-460.
        Examples are drawn from Chapman and Jonson.

A182   Hallett, Charles A. "The Satanic Nature of Volpone. "
        PQ, 49 (1970), 41-55.

A183   _____. "Jonson's Celia: A Reinterpretation of
        Volpone. " SP, 68 (1971), 50-69.
        "Celia, then, is the embodiment not of any one
        virtue but of a whole attitude toward life. Like
        the other characters in the play, she is a one-
        dimensional figure, the Heavenly One, no more
        psychologically complex than the crow or the
        raven. While we must admit that she is not one
        of the greatest dramatic heroines of the period,
        her nature being defined by quietude, which is in
        essence undramatic, we cannot deny that she has
        a very large and very important part to play in
        Volpone. Only if her role is fully understood can
        the vast scope of Jonson's vision be compre-
        hended" (p. 68).

A184   _____. "'Volpone' as the Source of the Sickroom
        Scheme in Middleton's 'Mad World.'" N&Q, N.S.
        18 (Jan. 1971), 24-25.

A185   Hamilton, Gary D. "Irony and Fortune in Sejanus. "
        SEL, 11 (1971), 265-281.
        Jonson's use of the concept of fortune is basic-
        ally ironic, implying that men can use this con-
        cept to avoid responsibility for actions which are
        merely expedient.

A186   Han, Pierre. "'Tabarine' in Ben Jonson's Volpone. "
        SCN, 28 (1970), 4-5.
        "It is most likely that, when alluding to Taba-
        rin, Jonson had in mind not an individual but a

whole tradition of improvised buffoonery that
characterized the Italian commedia dell'arte whose
influences were, of course, felt in France" (p. 5).

A187   Harris, Victor. "The Arts of Discourse in England,
        1500-1700." PQ, 37 (1958), 484-94.
        Milton and Jonson were Ramists, but they were
        not metaphysicals.

A188   Hart, Jeffrey. "Ben Jonson's Good Society: On the
        Growth of a Place and a Poem." Modern Age
        (Chicago), 7 (1963), 61-8.
        Concerning "To Penshurst": "Jonson was se-
        cure in his place at Penshurst because the social
        function of poetry was recognized. The Poet was
        the moral instructor of the governing class"
        (p. 64).

A189   Hartman, Jay H. "'Volpone' as a Possible Source
        for Melville's 'The Confidence Man.'" Susque-
        hanna Univ. Studies (Selinsgrove, Pa.), 7 (1965),
        247-60.

A190   Hawkins, Harriett. "The Idea of a Theatre in Jon-
        son's The New Inn." RenD, 9 (1966), 205-26.

A191   _____. "Jonson's Use of Traditional Dream
        Theory in The Vision of Delight." MP, 64 (1967),
        285-292.

A192   _____. "Folly, Incurable Disease, and Volpone."
        SEL, 8 (1968), 335-48.
        "Surely Jonson encourages the audience to rel-
        ish and, simultaneously, to recognize this folly,
        and to agree with Volpone when he states in the
        Epilogue that all the action, including the sen-
        tences, was entertaining. For through the organi-
        zation of scenes and the characterization, Jonson
        thematically sports with human crimes by reveal-
        ing them as manifestations of human folly, and by
        indicating dramatically their essentially absurd,
        self-defeating nature. Jonson distinguishes be-
        tween the innocuous fools and the vicious fools,
        but the difference is in degree of folly, not in
        kind. In Volpone, as in the Praise of Folly, the
        deceivers who are deceived ultimately themselves
        are presented as fit objects for the diversion and

(by way of it) the instruction of rational men"
(pp. 347-8).

A193   Hayashi, Tetsumaro. "Ben Johson [sic] and William
        Shakespeare: Their Relationship and Mutual Criti-
        cism. " EWR, 3 (1966-67), 23-47.

A194   Hays, H. R. "Satire and Identification: An Intro-
        duction to Ben Jonson. " KR, 19 (1957), 267-83.
            "Jonson's greatest creations are dramatizations
        of basic, unworthy human traits. We can un-
        doubtedly identify impulses within ourselves which
        parallel his portraits of lust, vanity, and selfish-
        ness, but the flagellant laughter which his situa-
        tions and exaggerations provoke never allows us
        any secret and greasy satisfaction" (p. 270).

A195   Heffner, Ray L. , Jr. "Unifying Symbols in the
        Comedy of Ben Jonson. " English Stage Comedy,
        ed. W. K. Wimsatt, Jr. , (Eng. Inst. Essays,
        1954), pp. 74-97.

A196   Held, George. "Jonson's Pindaric on Friendship. "
        CP, 3.1 (1970), 29-41.

A197   Hemphill, George. "Jonson's 'Fit of Rime Against
        Rime.' " Expl, 12 (1954), 50.
            In this poem rime presumably means "all the
        conventions of verse, particularly the modern
        ones. "

A198   Hibbard, G. R. "The Country House Poem of the
        Seventeenth Century. " JWCI, 19 (1956), 159-74.
            Perhaps the best article in English on the sub-
        ject drawing examples from Jonson, Carew, Her-
        rick and Marvell. "The marks of his [Jonson's]
        influence are to be seen in the constant references
        to architecture which occur in most of these
        poems (something that is not found in the Latin
        models), in the deep concern with the social func-
        tion of the great house [Penshurst] in the life of
        the community, and in the understanding of the
        reciprocal interplay of man and nature in the
        creation of a good life" (p. 159).

A199   _____ . "Goodness and Greatness: An Essay on
        the Tragedies of Ben Jonson and George Chap-

man." Renaissance and Modern Studies, 11 (1967),
5-54.

A200   Hill, Geoffrey. "The World's Proportion: Jonson's
       Dramatic Poetry in Sejanus and Catiline." Jaco-
       bean Theatre (Stratford-upon-Avon Studies, I).
       London: E. Arnold, 1960; New York: St. Mar-
       tin's Press, 1960, pp. 113-31.
       "In both Sejanus and Catiline, Jonson manages
       to blend a forthright dogmatism with astute trim-
       ming. This makes him, in a way, an epitome of
       the disturbed decades preceding the outbreak of
       the Civil War" (pp. 113-114).

A201   Hoffman, Gerhard. "Zur Form der satirischen
       Komödie: Ben Jonsons 'Volpone.'" Deutsche
       Vierteljahrs Schrift für Literaturwissenschaft und
       Geistesgeschichte (Stuttgart), 46 (1972), 1-27.

A202   Hollander, John. "Twelfth Night and the Morality of
       Indulgence." Sewanee Rev., 67 (1959), 220-238.
       Twelfth Night and Every Man In His Humour.

A203   Holleran, James V. "Character Transmutation in
       The Alchemist." College Lang. Assoc. Journal
       (Morgan State College, Balt.), 11 (1968), 221-7.

A204   Hollway, Morag. "Jonson's 'Proper Straine.'" CR,
       13 (1970), 51-67.

A205   Honig, Edwin. "Notes on Satire in Swift and Jon-
       son." New Mexico Quarterly Review, 18 (1948),
       155-63.

A206   _____. "Sejanus and Coriolanus: A Study in Ali-
       enation." MLQ, 12 (1951), 407-21.

A207   Horn, Robert D. "Shakespeare and Ben Jonson--
       Ashland, 1961." SQ, 12 (1961), 415-18.

A208   Horwich, Richard. "Hamlet and Eastward Ho."
       SEL, 11 (1971), 223-233.
       Considers Eastward Ho as an imitation and
       parody of Hamlet.

A209   Houck, J. K. "An Unidentified Borrowing in Jonson's
       Discoveries." N&Q, 15 (1968), 367-8.

A210   Howarth, Herbert.   "Falkland and Duppa's Jonsonus
        Virbius."   Expl, 17 (1958), No. 2, Item 11.
             Explicates the title of this volume.

A211   _____.   "Shakespeare's Gentleness."   ShS, 14
        (1961), 90-97.
             Attempts to explain why Ben Jonson refers to
        his contemporary as "My gentle Shakespeare."

A212   Hoy, Cyrus.   "The Shares of Fletcher and His Col-
        laborators in the Beaumont and Fletcher Canon."
        SB, 14 (1961), 45-67.
             The sixth installment of this article.   Chapman
        and Jonson may have had a hand in Rollo Duke of
        Normandy.

A213   _____.   "The Shares of Fletcher and His Collabo-
        rators in the Beaumont and Fletcher Canon."   SB,
        15 (1962), 71-90.
             The seventh installment of this article.   Fletch-
        er is sole author of 15 plays and collaborated with
        Beaumont, Massinger, and Jonson on the others.

A214   Hunter, G. K.   "English Folly and Italian Vice: The
        Moral Landscape of John Marston."   Jacobean
        Theatre (Stratford-upon-Avon Studies, 1), New
        York: St. Martin's Press, 1960; London: E. Ar-
        nold, 1960, pp. 85-111.
             Begins by comparing Every Man Out of His Hu-
        mour and Antonio and Mellida.

A215   Huntley, Frank L.   "Ben Jonson and Anthony Munday,
        or The Case Is Altered Altered Again."   PQ, 41
        (1962), 205-14.

A216   Hussey, Maurice.   "An Oath in 'The Alchemist.'"
        N&Q, 196 (1951), 433-4.
             Act I, ii--'By Gad' and 'By Jove.'

A217   _____.   "Ananias the Deacon: A Study of Religion
        in Jonson's The Alchemist."   English, 9 (1953),
        207-12.
             "What precisely Jonson's moral values were
        needs great clarification--we may say roughly
        that standards were set by Jonson's adherence to
        the Catholic Church and were, in dramatic terms,
        closely related to the Morality Play" (p. 208).

A218 Hutchison, Barbara. "Ben Jonson's 'Let Me Be What
      I Am': An Apology in Disguise." ELN, 2 (1965),
      185-90.
          "It is an apology for poetry, really, which
      grows out of an effort on Jonson's part to explain
      himself and the kind of poetry he writes. By
      speaking for himself in the poem as a poet, Jon-
      son has made it clear, I think, that he intends to
      discuss poetry as art; however, although he has
      discarded his private affairs, he does not subse-
      quently divorce poetry from a moral context"
      (p. 186).

A219 Inglis, Fred. "Classicism and Poetic Drama." EIC,
      16 (1966), 154-69.
          Contrasted to Shakespeare, Jonson's classical
      training limits the possibilities of his poetic achieve-
      ment.

A220 Janicka, Irena. "Jonson's Staple of News: Sources
      and Traditional Devices." Kwartalnik Neofilo-
      logiczny (Warsaw), 15 (1968), 301-7.

A221 _____. "The Popular Background of Ben Jonson's
      Masques." SJW, 105 (1969), 183-208.
          Treats Jonson's masques (Pleasure Reconciled,
      e.g.) in the light of earlier traditions. Illustrated.

A222 John, Lisle Cecil. "Ben Jonson's Epigram CXIV to
      Mistress Philip Sydney." JEGP, 45 (1946), 214-7.
          This epigram is addressed to Philip (not Philip-
      pa), the daughter of Robert Sidney, Earl of Lei-
      cester.

A223 _____. "Ben Jonson's 'To Sir William Sydney, on
      his Birthday.'" MLR, 52 (1957), 168-76.

A224 Johnston, George B. "Ben Jonson of Gresham Col-
      lege." TLS, Dec. 28, 1951, p. 837.
          Cf. C. J. Sisson, "Ben Jonson of Gresham
      College," TLS, 21 Sept. 1951, p. 604 (see A403).
      Jonson's lament in "Execration upon Vulcan" cor-
      roborates Sisson's theory because Jonson needed
      Art of Poetry, Grammar, and Discoveries for his
      lecture notes lost in the fire of 1623.

A225 _____. "'An Epistle Mendicant' by Ben Jonson."

N&Q, N. S. 1 (1954), 471.
   Notes the same figure of wants as moles or un-
derminers in Jonson's petition in verse to Lord
Weston, Lord High Treasurer, 1631, and in the
dream-fable sent to the Earl of New Castle, 20th
Dec., the same year.

A226   . "Jonson's 'Perseus Upon Pegasus.'" RES,
       6 (1955), 65-7.
            See also John D. Reeves, RES, 6 (1955), 397-9,
       a follow-up note where he deals only with Peele
       and Heywood.

A227   . "An Apocryphal Jonsonian Epigram."
       N&Q, N. S. 5 (1958), 543-4.

A228   Jones, Myrddin. "Sir Epicure Mammon: A Study in
       Spiritual Fornication." RenQ, 22 (1969), 233-242.
            This article "makes detailed and precise use of
       I Kings and of the Homilies in examining Mam-
       mon's language, and in convicting Mammon as an-
       tichrist" (YWES).

A229   Jones, Robert C. "The Satirist's Retirement in Jon-
       son's 'Apologetical Dialogue.'" ELH, 34 (1967),
       447-67.

A230   [no entry]

A231   Jungnell, Tore. "Notes on the Language of Ben Jon-
       son." Studier i Modern Sprakvetenskap (Stock-
       holm), N. S. 1 (1960), 86-110.

A232   Kaplan, Joel H. "Dramatic and Moral Energy in
       Ben Jonson's Bartholomew Fair." RenD, N. S. 3
       (1970), 137-156.
            "In Bartholomew Fair the same skepticism
       towards extravagant energy and mimesis that ap-
       pears in both Volpone and The Alchemist is brought
       to bear upon the roaring spirit of Smithfield, re-
       vealing a grotesque turbulence that coarsens as it
       liberates, creating tumult and heightening antago-
       nisms while moving characters towards a recon-
       ciliation at the level of flesh and blood, where all
       are united by a common participation in human
       folly" (p. 141).

A233   Kay, W. David. "The Shaping of Ben Jonson's Ca-
       reer: A Reexamination of Facts and Problems."
       MP, 67 (1970), 224-37.

A234   _____. "The Christian Wisdom of Ben Jonson's
       'On My First Sonne.'" SEL, 11 (1971), 125-136.
       "As is frequently the case in Jonson's poetry,
       the underlying attitudes which give the conclusion
       its point are almost obscured by the deceptive
       plainness of his metaphors and the restraint of his
       tone, yet they are accessible if we do not mistake
       the simplicity of language for simplicity of thought.
       To support the interpretation outlined above, it
       will be useful to reexamine the development of the
       poem, invoking the aid of Jonson's other poetry,
       his source in Martial, and some analogous pas-
       sages from the works of St. Augustine to clarify
       Jonson's religious perspective on human love"
       (p. 129).

A235   Keast, W. R. "Some Seventeenth-Century Allusions
       to Shakespeare and Jonson." N&Q, 194 (1949),
       468-9.

A236   Kennedy-Skipton, A. L. D. "A Footnote to 'John
       Ward and Restoration Drama.'" SQ, 12 (1961),
       353.

A237   Kermode, J. F. "The Banquet of Sense." Bul. John
       Ryland's Lib., 44 (1961), 68-99.
       Traces the theme of the Banquet of Sense from
       its Christian and pagan sources into its appearance
       in pictorial art of the Netherlands [with special
       reference to Adrien Collaert] and into Ben Jon-
       son's The New Inn and Chapman's Ouids Banquet
       of Sence, among others.

A238   Kifer, Devra Rowland. "The Staple of News: Jon-
       son's Festive Comedy." SEL, 12 (1972), 329-344.
       Play should be viewed as a festive comedy
       structured as a morality account of the salvation
       of Pennyboy Jr.

A239   Kim, Seyong. "Ben Jonson the Playwright." The
       English Lang. and Literature (Eng. Lit. Soc. of
       Korea), No. 5 (1958), pp. 28-50.

A240   Kirby, Thomas A. "The Triple Tun." MLN, 62

(1947), 191-2.
In "Herrick's generous lines to Ben Jonson" identifies the 'Triple Tun' as the 'Three Tuns' (or Tonnes) in Bankside.

A241 _____. "'The Triple Tun' Again." MLN, 63 (1948), 56-7.
Further discussion of the size and appointments of Jonson's famous tavern.

A242 Kirchner, Gustav. "Die Weltgeltung Shakespeares." SJ, 101 (1965).
Closes with Jonson's lines contributed to the First Folio, translated into German.

A243 Kliegman, Benjamine. "A 'Jonson-Shakespeare' Portrait." ShN, 2 (1952), 35.

A244 Knoll, Robert E. "How to Read The Alchemist." CE, 21 (1960), 456-60.
"The Alchemist is essentially a Christian play. Jonson is here concerned with showing how false gods may usurp the very name and ritual of the true God. His play deals with religious perversions" (p. 459).

A245 Kranidas, Thomas. "Possible Revisions or Additions in Jonson's Epicoene." Anglia, 83 (1965), 451-3.

A246 Krishnamurthi, M. G. "The Ethical Basis of Ben Jonson's Plays." Journal of the Maharaja Sayajirao University of Baroda, 11.1 (1962), 139-57.

A247 LaFrance, Marston. "Fielding's Use of the 'Humor' Tradition." Bucknell Review, 17.3 (1969), 53-63.
Traces the tradition back to Jonson.

A248 LaRegina, Gabriella. "Ben Jonson e la sua fortuna nel Seicento." EM, 16 (1965), 37-86.

A249 Lascelles, Mary. "Shakespeare's Comic Insight." Proceedings of the British Academy, 48 (1962), 171-86.
Contrasts Shakespeare's comedy with Jonson's.

A250 Latham, Jacqueline E. M. "Form in Bartholomew Fair." English, 21 (1972), 8-11.

"My purpose is to discuss more fully the relationship between the microcosm of the puppets and
the macrocosm of the play" (p. 8).

A251   Lavin, J. A.   "Printers for Seven Jonson Quartos,"
The Library, Ser. 5, 25.4 (Dec. 1970), 331-338.
In some cases seeks to identify printers of Jonson quartos, in others to correct printers inaccu-
rately identified.   The printer of Q1 EMO (1600)
was not Richard Braddock, as Greg tentatively asserts (and Herford and Simpson follow Greg here--
Works, 9 [1950], 9) but Adam Islip.   Q1 of EMI
(1601) was printed by Simon Stafford.   Ornament
evidence also points to Richard Read as the printer of Cynthia's Revels Q1 (1601), and to George
Eld as the printer of Volpone Q1 (1607).   Eld is
also named in this essay as the printer of The
Masque of Blackness (1608) and of Jonson's part
of The King's Entertainment Through The City of
London (1604) "despite the imprint 'Printed at London by V. S. for Edward Blount.'"   Finally, Lavin confirms Greg's tentative identification of
Richard Braddock as the printer of Q1 Poetaster
(1602).

A252   Law, Richard A.   "'Sejanus' in 'the wolves black
jaw.'" Penna. Council of Teachers of English
Bulletin, No. 15 (1967), 27-40.

A253   Lee, Umphrey.   "Jonson's Bartholomew Fair and the
Popular Dramatic Tradition." The Louisburg College Journal of Arts and Sciences, 1 (1967), 6-16.

A254   Legatt, Alexander.   "The Suicide of Volpone." UTQ,
39 (1969), 19-32.
Examines Volpone and the nature of his self-
enlightenment.   Volpone "'destroys himself, not
because he gets careless or his luck runs out at
the beginning of Act V, but because of an impulse
deeply rooted in his nature'; this is not 'simply
overreaching' as with Mosca's case, but something
more complex: indeed Volpone is seen as having
an 'instinct to bring his own play to an end'"
(YWES).

A255   Lemay, J. A. Leo.   "Jonson and Milton: Two Influences in Oakes's Elegie." NEQ, 38 (1965), 90-2.

A256   Levin, Harry. "Two Magian Comedies: The Tem-
        pest and The Alchemist." ShS, 22 (1969), 47-58.
            Examines the two plays on the basis of their
        closely related themes, esp. natural magic and
        illusion.

A257   Levin, Lawrence L. "Justice and Society in Sejanus
        and Volpone." Discourse, 13 (1970), 319-24.

A258   _____. "Clement Justice in Every Man in His
        Humor." SEL, 12 (1972), 291-307.
            Clement plays roles of priest, educator, and
        poet reformer, and identifies himself with Jonson.
        With the creation of Clement Jonson deviates from
        the Elizabethan convention of the dull-witted jus-
        tice of the peace and produces a new type of magis-
        trate and a prototype for particular characters in
        the next four plays.

A259   Levin, Richard. "The Staple of News, the Society of
        Jeerers, and Canters' College." PQ, 44 (1965),
        445-53.
            Provides a structural analysis of the play.

A260   _____. "The Structure of Bartholomew Fair."
        PMLA, 80 (1965), 172-9.

A261   _____. "'The Ass in Compound': A Lost Pun in
        Middleton, Ford, and Jonson." ELN, 4 (1966),
        12-15.

A262   _____. "Some Second Thoughts on Central
        Themes." MLR, 67 (1972), 1-10.
            Includes comments on Volpone.

A263   _____. "The New New Inn and The Proliferation
        of Good Bad Drama." EIC, 22 (Jan. 1972), 41-47.
            Considers The New Inn "simply a bad play,"
        not a parody of one.

A264   _____. "Thematic Unity and the Homogenization
        of Character." MLQ, 33 (1972), 23-29.
            Includes discussion of Volpone, The Alchemist,
        and Bartholomew Fair.

A265   Lindsay, Barbara N. "The Structure of Tragedy in
        Sejanus." ES (Anglo-Amer. Supp.), 1969, xliv-1.

A266   Litt, Dorothy E. "Unity of Theme in Volpone."
        BNYPL, 73 (1969), 218-26.

A267   Lodge, Oliver. "A Ben Jonson Puzzle." TLS, Sept.
        13, 1947, p. 465.
        Suggests that Jonson changed Cis to Pry (The
        New Inn) to avoid the sound of hissing instead of
        to avoid a personal allusion.

A268   McCullen, Joseph T., Jr. "Conference with the
        Queen of Fairies: A Study of Jonson's Workman-
        ship in The Alchemist." Studia Neophilologica, 23
        (1951), 87-95.

A269   McCutcheon, Elizabeth. "Jonson's 'To Penshurst,'
        36." Expl, 25 (1967), No. 52.
        "Officiously," line 36, is a pun.

A270   McDiarmid, Matthew P. "The Stage Quarrel in Wily
        Beguiled." N&Q, N.S. 3(1956), 380-3.
        The play refers to the 'poetomachia' waged by
        Jonson with Marston and Dekker.

A271   McDonald, Charles O. "Restoration Comedy as
        Drama of Satire: An Investigation into Seventeenth-
        Century Aesthetics." SP, 61 (1964), 522-44.
        Best Restoration comedy has a consistent aes-
        thetic derived from classical teaching, Jonson, and
        Hobbes.

A272   McElroy, D. "The 'Artificiall Sea' in Jonson's
        'Masque of Blacknesse.'" N&Q, N.S. 7 (1960),
        419-21.

A273   _____. "The Falling 'Curtain' in Jonson's 'Masque
        of Blacknesse.'" N&Q, N.S. 7 (1960), 174-5.

A274   McEuen, Kathryn A. "Jonson and Juvenal." RES,
        21 (1945), 92-104.

A275   McFarland, Ronald E. "Jonson's Magnetic Lady and
        the Reception of Gilbert's De Magnete." SEL, 11
        (1971), 283-93.
        "It is the employment of the magnetic conceit
        that gives the drama its compact and coherent
        structure which is, at last, its sole recommenda-
        tion" (p. 293).

A276 _____. "Jonson's Epigrams, XI ('On Some-Thing
      That Walkes Some-Where'). " Expl, 31 (Dec.
      1972), No. 26.

A277 McGalliard, John C. "Chaucerian Comedy: The
      Merchant's Tale, Jonson, and Molière. " PQ, 25
      (1946), 343-70.

A278 McGinnis, Paul J. "Ben Jonson's Discoveries. "
      N&Q, N. S. 4 (1957), 162-3.

A279 _____. "Ben Jonson on Savile's Tacitus. " Classi-
      cal Journal, 55 (1959), 120-21.

A280 McGlinchee, Claire. "'Still Harping....'" ShQ, 6
      (1955), 362-4.
          Finds a parallel to Polonius' fatherly advice in
      Knowell's speech to Stephen his nephew (Everyman
      In, I. i); see Josephine Waters Bennett. "Char-
      acterization in Polonius' Advice to Laertes. " ShQ,
      4 (1953), 3-9; R. H. Bowers, ShQ, 4 (1953), 362-
      4.

A281 McKenzie, D. F. "The Printer of the Third Volume
      of Jonson's Workes (1640). " SB, 25 (1972), 177-
      78.
          "That the printer was John Dawson Junior may
      be proved on the evidence of one factotum depict-
      ing Salome receiving the head of John the Baptist,
      and two uppercase, French Canon 'H's. ' Their
      combined testimony removes all doubt" (p. 177).

A282 McKenzie, James. "Jonson's 'Elizabeth, L. H.'"
      N&Q, N. S. 9 (1962), 210.
          "Elizabeth, L. H., " McKenzie speculates, is
      Lady Hunsdon, née Elizabeth Spencer of Althorp.

A283 Mackin, Cooper R. "The Satiric Technique of John
      Oldham's Satyrs upon the Jesuits. " SP, 62 (1965),
      78-90.
          Discusses Oldham's development of older satiri-
      cal models, in particular Jonson's Catiline.

A284 McMillin, Scott. "Jonson's Early Entertainments:
      New Information from Hatfield House. " RenD,
      N. S. 1 (1968), 153-166.

A285   McNeal, Thomas H.   "Every Man Out of his Humour
       and Shakespeare's Sonnets." N&Q, 197 (1952),
       376.

A286   McPherson, David.   "Some Renaissance Sources for
       Jonson's Early Comic Theory." ELN, 8 (1971),
       180-82.
       Scaliger and Minturno.

A287   Mager, Don.   "The Paradox of Tone in Bartholomew
       Fayre." Thoth (Dept. of English, Syracuse Univ.),
       9 (1968), 39-47.

A288   Main, C. F.   "Two Items in the Jonson Apocrypha."
       N&Q, N.S. 1 (1954), 243-5.
       Discusses the reason for Peter Whalley's attri-
       bution to Jonson of Browne's epitaph on the
       Countess of Pembroke and the vicissitudes in the
       printing of its second stanza; believes the epitaph
       on the honest lawyer may be Jonson's.

A289   _____.   "Ben Jonson and an Unknown Poet on the
       King's Senses." MLN, 74 (1959), 389-93.
       Concerning The Gypsies Metamorphosed, 11.
       1327-85; the "unknown poet" responsible for the
       parody of Jonson's lines (c. 1621) is tentatively
       identified as James Johnson; Alexander Gill the
       Younger and William Drummond are ruled out.

A290   Main, William W.   "'Insula Fortunata' in Jonson's
       'Every Man Out of His Humour.'" N&Q, N.S. 1
       (1954), 197-8.
       Jonson follows a tradition in choosing the Iland
       to signify the land of fools: Erasmus' Moriae
       encomium, well known to Jonson, describes the
       Fortunate Isles as the birthplace of folly herself.

A291   _____.   "Dramaturgical Norms in Elizabethan
       Repertory." SP, 54 (1957), 128-48.
       Deals with plot analysis in seventy-six plays
       usually dated 1598-1602.

A292   Major, John M.   "Milton's View of Rhetoric." SP,
       64 (1967), 685-711.
       Regarding the influence of Plato, Augustine,
       Bacon, and Jonson.

A293   Marotti, Arthur F. "The Self-Reflexive Art of Ben
        Jonson's Sejanus." TSLL, 12 (1970), 197-220.
            "It is my contention that Sejanus' antitragic
        character is shaped largely by Jonson's over-
        indulgence in self-conscious artifice" (p. 197).

A294   _____. "All About Jonson's Poetry." ELH, 39
        (1972), 208-237.
            "Looking at this larger body of verse, we can,
        I think, better perceive Jonson's stylistic virtuosity,
        the way his poetry ranges between extremes of
        copiousness and restraint. Although I intend the
        remarks in the following pages to be critically
        descriptive rather than prescriptive (I am not so much
        interested in proving a thesis as re-exploring Jon-
        son's work with open eyes), my focal points are
        two kinds of verse Jonson composed--the first a
        poetry of explosive imagery and perverse imagining,
        the second a poetry of more visible control, imag-
        istically spare, prosodically tight, and intellectual-
        ly lucid. Jonson is an artistic schizophrenic, with
        both a Dionysian and Apollonian side" (p. 209).

A295   Maxwell, J. C. "Comic Mispunctuation in Every Man
        in His Humour." ES, 33 (1952), 218-19.

A296   _____. "The Poems of Herrick?" N&Q, N.S. 2
        (1955), 500.
            Lines that Howarth ["Two Poems of Herrick?"
        N&Q, N.S. 2 (1955), 380-1] ascribes to Herrick,
        Maxwell attributes to Jonson in opening lines of
        Act V of Sejanus.

A297   _____. "The Relation of Macbeth to Sophonisba."
        N&Q, N.S. 2 (1955), 374-5.
            Sees a reflection of Sejanus in Sophonisba, and
        a parallel to that in Macbeth.

A298   May, Louis F. "Jonson's 'Epitaph on Solomon Pavy.'"
        Expl, 20:2 (1961), Item 16.
            This poem derives from "the tradition of the
        puer senex topos."

A299   Meagher, John Carney. "The Dance and the Masques
        of Ben Jonson." JWCI, 25 (1962), 258-77.

A300   Meier, T. "The Naming of Characters in Jonson's

Comedies." Eng. Studies in Africa (Johannesburg),
7.1 (1964), 88-95.

A301   Merchant, Paul. "Another Misprint in Epicoene?"
The Library, 5th Ser. 27:4 (Dec. 1972), 326.
Wishes to go against the authority of the 1616
Folio and emend the phrase "a brace of fat Does"
in La Foole's lines at I. iv. 46 to "a brace of fat
Doues."

A302   Miller, Joyce. "Volpone: A Study of Dramatic Am-
biguity." Studies in English Language and Literature, ed. Alice Shalvi and A. A. Mendilow. Jeru-
salem: The Hebrew Univ., 1966, pp. 35-95.

A303   Mills, Lloyd L. "A Clarification of Broker's Use of
'A Perfect Sanguine' in The Staple of News."
N&Q, 14 (1967), 208-9.

A304   _____. "Barish's 'The Double Plot' Supplemented:
The Tortoise Symbolism." Serif, 4.3 (1967), 25-
8.
Concerns Volpone, V. iv.

A305   _____. "Ben Jonson's Poetry: A Caveat and Two
Interpretations." The New Laurel Review (Penning-
ton, N.J.), 1 (1971), 30-34.
Analysis of "On My First Son" and Epigram
LXXXI.

A306   Moloney, Michael F. "The Prosody of Milton's Epitaph, L'Allegro, and Il Penseroso." MLN, 72
(1957), 174-8.
Finds in Epitaph on the Marchioness of Winchester
a solemn meter in the manner of Ben Jonson.

A307   Murphy, Avon Jack. "The Critical Elegy of Earlier
Seventeenth-Century England." Genre, 5 (1972),
75-97.
Includes discussion of Jonson.

A308   Murray, W. A. "What Was the Soul of the Apple?"
RES, 10 (1959), 141-55.
Offers a new interpretation of Metempsychosis,
which he contends has been misunderstood, and to
which Jonson is not a good guide.

A309   _____. "Ben Jonson and Dr. Mayerne." TLS,
            Sept. 2, 1960, p. 561.

A310   Murrin, Michael. "Poetry as Literary Criticism."
        MP, 65 (1968), 202-7.
            Places Cowley's ode "Of Wit" in the context of
        earlier such 'Mirror' poems by Carew, Jonson,
        Donne, and Herbert.

A311   Nania, Anthony J. "Addenda: Ben Jonson: A Check-
        list of Editions, Biography, and Criticism, 1947-
        1964." Research Opportunities in Renaissance
        Drama, 10 (1967), 32.

A312   Nash, Ralph. "Milton, Jonson, and Tiberius."
        Classical Philology, 41 (1946), 164.
            Milton got the Tiberian allusion in RCG from
        Jonson.

A313   _____. "The Comic Intent of Volpone." SP, 44
            (1947), 26-40.
            "This amount of subordinate comedy in Volpone,
        coupled with the comic treatment of the gulls, sug-
        gests that the effect of the play, at least up to the
        second trial scene, should be far from that of
        tragic foreboding" (p. 40).

A314   _____. "The Parting Scene in Jonson's Poetaster
            (IV, ix)." PQ, 31 (1952), 54-62.

A315   _____. "Ben Jonson's Tragic Poems." SP, 55
            (1958), 164-86.
            "Non-Aristotelian and non-Shakespearean, these
        tragedies possess remarkable qualities that give
        them distinction among their contemporaries and
        ought to make them well known in English drama.
        Their boldness of design and freshness of tech-
        nique, impressive to Jonson's contemporary ad-
        mirers, should not be lost for us under a depress-
        ing label of 'early attempts at neo-classicism.'
        If the design and technique have come to pretty
        much a dead end, with little influence historically,
        this is often the fate of those intelligent experi-
        ments that help to keep a literature alive" (p. 164).

A316   Nevo, Ruth. "The Masque of Greatness." ShStud,
        3 (1967), 111-128.

Notes the "startling" resemblance between Cleopatra's dream of Antony in Shakespeare and Jonson's Masque of Hymen.

A317   Nicoll, Allardyce.   "Shakespeare and the Court
       Masque." SJ, 94 (1958), 51-62.
       Discusses influence of early masques--especially
       Jonson's--on Shakespeare.

A318   Northcote-Bade, Kirsty.   "The Play of Illusion in Ben
       Jonson's Comedies." Words: Wai-Te-Ata Studies
       in Literature, No. 2 (December 1966), p. 82-91.

A319   Nosworthy, J. M.   "The Case Is Altered." JEGP,
       51 (1952), 61-70.
       The play was written in collaboration with Porter
       and Chettle, and is to be identified with the play
       called Hot Anger Soon Cold by Henslowe.

A320   _____. "Marlowe's Ovid and Davies's Epigrams--
       A Postscript." RES, N.S. 15 (1964), 397-8.
       Jonson's possible influence on the publication of
       the octavos at Middleburg.

A321   O'Connor, Daniel.   "Jonson's 'A Hymne to God the
       Father.'" N&Q, N.S. 12 (1965), 379-80.
       Perhaps John Posin's A Collection of Private
       Devotions (1627) contains an early version of Jon-
       son's poem which supposedly first appeared in the
       Folio of 1640.

A322   O'Donnell, Norbert F.   "The Authorship of The Care-
       less Shepherdess." PQ, 33 (1954), 43-47.
       A possible source for Jonson's The Sad Shep-
       herd; Jonson may have seen a manuscript of the
       earlier Careless Shepherdess.

A323   Olive, W. J.   "A Chaucer Allusion in Jonson's Bar-
       tholomew Fair." MLQ, 13 (1952), 21-2.
       In II, iv of Bartholomew Fair, and in III, iv of
       The Magnetic Lady.

A324   Orgel, Stephen.   "To Make Boards to Speak: Inigo
       Jones's Stage and the Jonsonian Masque." RenD,
       N.S. 1 (1968), 121-152.

A325   Ornstein, Robert.   "The Ethical Design of The Re-

venger's Tragedy." ELH, 21 (1954), 81-93.
The ethical design is similar to that of Volpone.

A326   . "Volpone and Renaissance Psychology."
N&Q, N.S. 3 (1956), 471-2.

A327   . "Shakespearian and Jonsonian Comedy."
ShS, 22 (1969), 43-46.
Against Shakespeare's romantic comedy, Jonson's satiric comedy is negative and sometimes
repelling.

A328   Osborn, James M. "Ben Jonson and the Eccentric
Lord Stanhope." TLS, Jan. 4, 1957, p. 16.
Concerning Lord Stanhope's marginal notes in
his copy of the 1640 Folio. Cf. TLS, Oct. 11,
1957, p. 609, where R. A. Sayce describes
another book annotated by Stanhope.

A329   Osgood, Charles G. "Epithalamion and Prothalamion:
'and theyr eccho ring.'" MLN, 76 (1961), 205-8.
The Spenserian influence on 17th century epi-
thalamists, including Jonson.

A330   Papajewski, Helmut. "Ben Jonsons Laudatio auf
Shakespeare: Kategorien des literarischen Urteils
in der Renaissance." Poetica, 1 (1967), 483-507.

A331   Parfitt, G. A. E. "The Poetry of Ben Jonson."
EIC, 18 (1968), 18-31.

A332   . "The Poetry of Thomas Carew." Renaissance and Modern Studies, 12 (1968), 56-67.
Carew is comparable to Jonson in his response
to the breadth of experience, as well as stylis-
tically.

A333   . "Ethical Thought and Ben Jonson's Poetry."
SEL, 9 (1969), 123-34.
What makes Jonson's poetry distinctive is the
centrality of a consistent ethical position which is
socially rather than religiously biased.

A334   . "Compromise Classicism: Language and
Rhythm in Ben Jonson's Poetry." SEL, 11 (1971),
109-23.
Analyzes Jonson's poetic style in light of the

sixteenth-century English plain style and suggests
that certain features of his style may be related
to aspects of Latin verse.

A335 _____. "Volpone." EIC, 21 (1971), 411-12.
Reply to Donaldson [EIC, 21 (1971), 121-34],
analyzing characters of Celia and Bonario in the
play.

A336 Parker, R. B. "The Themes and Staging of Bartholomew Fair." UTQ, 39 (1970), 293-309.
"The puppet show is within a fair which is within a bear-baiting theatre, which is within a greedy,
quarrelsome, childish world; and Jonson, like the
superb stage artist he is, explores their analogies
with his theatre, his company, and his particular,
popular audience constantly in mind" (p. 306).

A337 Parr, Johnstone. "Non-Alchemical Pseudo-Sciences
in The Alchemist." PQ, 24 (1945), 85-9.

A338 _____. "A Note on Jonson's The Staple of News."
MLN, 60 (1945), 117.
Concerns the allusion in Act IV to the influence
of "Hercules Starre."

A339 Parsons, D. S. J. "The Odes of Drayton and Jonson." QQ, 75 (1968), 675-84.
The exalted tone of the ode could only be main-
tained with great difficulty in the unheroic Jacobean age.

A340 Partridge, A. C. "The Periphrastic Auxiliary Verb
'Do' and Its Use in the Plays of Ben Jonson."
MLR, 43 (1948), 26-33.

A341 _____. "Shakespeare's Orthography in Venus and
Adonis and Some Early Quartos." ShS, No. 7
(1954), 35-47.
Jonson's influence on Shakespeare's orthography.

A342 Partridge, Edward B. "The Allusiveness of Epicoene."
ELH, 22 (1955), 93-107.
Violations of contemporary standards of de-
corum provide the comedy.

A343 _____. "A Crux in Jonson's The New Inne."

MLN, 71 (1956), 168-70.
> Explains the passage V. ii. 15-16 as humor by
> Jonson rather than as a bit of obscure folklore.

A344   . "The Symbolism of Clothes in Jonson's
Last Plays. " JEGP, 56 (1957), 396-409.

A345   . "Ben Jonson: The Makings of the Dramatist (1596-1602). " Elizabethan Theatre (Stratford-
upon-Avon Studies, 9), London: E. Arnold, 1966,
pp. 221-44.

A346   Peery, William. "The Influence of Ben Jonson on
Nathan Field. " SP, 43 (1946), 482-97.

A347   . "Eastward Ho! and A Woman Is A Weather-
cock. " MLN, 62 (1947), 131-2.
> A Jonsonian echo in Field's play.

A348   Peltz, Catharine W. "Thomas Campion, an Elizabethan Neo-Classicist. " MLQ, 11 (1950), 3-6.
> Jonson's lyrics overshadowed Campion's.

A349   Petronella, Vincent F. "Jonson's Bartholomew Fair:
A Study in Baroque Style. " Discourse, 13 (1970),
325-37.
> Analyzes the play in the light of Barish's notion
> of baroque prose style as a clashing of symmetry
> with asymmetry.

A350   . "Teaching Ben Jonson's The Alchemist,
Alchemy and Analysis. " HAB, 21.2 (1970), 19-23.

A351   Phialas, Peter G. "Comic Truth in Shakespeare and
Jonson. " SAQ, 62 (1963), 78-91.

A352   Pineas, Rainer. "The Morality Vice in Volpone. "
Discourse, 5 (1962), 451-59.

A353   Piper, William B. "The Inception of the Closed
Heroic Couplet. " MP, 66 (1969), 306-21.
> The English heroic couplet especially as in-
> fluenced by Marlowe and Jonson.

A354   Plumstead, A. W. "Satirical Parody in Roister
Doister: A Reinterpretation. " SP, 60 (1963),
141-54.

Discusses, in part, "a dimension of irony that looks forward to Jonson."

A355   Potter, John M. "Old Comedy in Bartholomew Fair." Criticism, 10 (1968), 290-99.
"Jonson's development of the structure of the play around the four events of Old Comedy (the parabasis to express the author's position, the feast of communion, the agon debating the theme, and the final exodos of a marriage feast which creates a new society), his use of a series of illustrative episodes related directly to the theme rather than to each other, the choice of an old man as hero, the anti-romanticism, and the use of Aristophanic language, names, and incidents indicate that Jonson was not writing a sloppy exercise in New Comedy, but was consciously trying to adapt the form of Old Comedy to the Jacobean stage. He succeeded admirably" (p. 299).

A356   Potts, Abbie Findlay. "Cynthia's Revels, Poetaster, and Troilus and Cressida." ShQ, 5 (1954), 297-302.
Troilus echoes Jonsonian devices in Cynthia's Revels and the Poetaster; such echoes may help to interpret puzzling passages in Shakespeare's play.

A357   Potts, L. J. "Ben Jonson and the Seventeenth Century." ES, N.S. 2 (1949), 7-24.
"Where Sidney distorts Aristotle's theory [of poetry and the poet], Jonson interprets it correctly, because he was quite prepared to make poetry the handmaid of science; and that was because he was a whole-hearted Baconian" (p. 18).

A358   Putney, Rufus. "Jonson's Poetic Comedy." PQ, 41 (1962), 188-204.
The discussion mainly concerns theatrical matters.

A359   _____. "'This So Subtile Sport': Some Aspects of Jonson's Epigrams." University of Colorado Studies. Series in Lang. and Lit., 10 (1966), pp. 37-56.
"So various was Jonson's poetic output that no generalization can encompass it all, unless it be

that the writing of his poetry and the appreciation
of it is indeed a 'subtle sport' " (p. 37).

A360   Race, Sidney. "Harleian MS. 6395 and Its Editor."
        N&Q, N. S. 4 (1957), 77-9.
            The MS. tells of Shakespeare's acting as a god-
        father to one of Jonson's children.

A361   Rackin, Phyllis. "Poetry Without Paradox: Jonson's
        'Hymne' to Cynthia." Criticism, 4 (1962), 186-96.
            "What I am arguing is that if the demand for
        Decorum (or for any other quality, however irrele-
        vant to the aesthetic success of a work) can modi-
        fy (if not altogether eliminate) the operation of the
        demand for paradox, and if the poem is a success-
        ful one, then the demand for paradox cannot be
        regarded as an essential basis of aesthetic judg-
        ment" (p. 196).

A362   Rathmell, J. C. A. "Jonson, Lord Lisle, and Pens-
        hurst." ELR, 1:3 (Autumn 1971), 250-60.
            "If we read "To Penshurst" in the light of ...
        contemporary evidence regarding Lord Lisle's do-
        mestic affairs, two main facts emerge. However
        much Jonson is indebted to literary precedents,
        the poem is also firmly grounded in Jonson's inti-
        mate knowledge of the Sidney family.... The dis-
        tinguishing characteristics of the Penshurst house-
        hold, as Jonson presents it, are the warmth of its
        hospitality, the generosity and humanity of its
        owners, and its importance as the focus of the
        local community. Jonson deliberately emphasizes
        the fact that the bounty of the estate proceeds from
        the humanity rather than the lavishness of the wel-
        come provided by its lord and lady; the bonds that
        cement the Sidney family, he suggests, are paral-
        leled by the close ties that link the tenants to
        their master and the house to its natural surround-
        ings. In each case it is the health and naturalness
        of the relationship that Jonson celebrates" (pp. 259-
        60).

A363   Redding, David C. "A Note on Jonson Attribution."
        N&Q, N. S. 7 (1960), 52-3.
            Shadwell did not invent the couplet translated
        "In a Dish came Fish ..." in Ben Jonson's Jests
        (Herford and Simpson, 8, 424).

A364 Redwine, James D., Jr. "Beyond Psychology: The Moral Basis of Jonson's Theory of Humour Characterization." ELH, 28 (1961), 316-34.
"In the strictest sense, then, a Jonsonian humour is not simply an abnormal psychological condition; ultimately, it is that evil moral condition that occurs when man's carnal appetite gains ascendency over his reason" (p. 330).

A365 Reed, Robert R., Jr. "Ben Jonson's Pioneering in Sentimental Comedy." N&Q, 195 (June 1950), 272-3.
The essay deals with the subplot of The Devil Is an Ass.

A366 Reiman, Donald H. "Marston, Jonson, and the 'Spanish Tragedy' Additions." N&Q, N.S. 7 (1960), 336-7.
The fact that Poetaster, III. ii. 230-5, 1602Q, is a parody of Marston's Antonio's Revenge, V. iii. 1-4, supports the view that the extant additions to S.T. "are earlier than those for which Jonson was paid by Henslowe in 1601-2."

A367 Rexroth, Kenneth. "The Works of Ben Jonson." Sat. Rev., Dec. 17, 1966, p. 25.

A368 Reyburn, Marjorie L. "New Facts and Theories about the Parnassus Plays." PMLA, 74 (1959), 325-35.
Uses internal evidence to reveal the Cambridge playwrights' satire of Jonson.

A369 Ricks, Christopher. "Sejanus and Dismemberment." MLN, 76 (1961), 301-8.
"The following note points out that in its imagery--the imagery of the parts of the body--the play anticipates and works towards the final scene. For not only is Sejanus dismembered, but the play shows the tragic dislocation of Roman life, the dismemberment of the body politic" (p. 301).

A370 Robinson, James E. "Bartholomew Fair: Comedy of Vapors." SEL, 1.2 (1961), 65-80.
"I propose to show that the center of the structure and meaning of Bartholomew Fair lies in the

symbolism of vapors that pervades the play's
imagery, characterization, and action. To explain
the play as a comedy of vapors is to explain how
the play is designed to fulfill classical concepts of
dramatic unity, verisimilitude, and the function of
comedy. The purpose of comedy, according to
any good Renaissance classicist, was to imitate
the manners of men in order to hold up the mir-
ror to the ridiculous in human nature and therefore instruct as well as delight" (p. 66).

A371   Rollin, Roger B. "Images of Libertinism in Every
       Man in His Humor and 'To his Coy Mistress.'"
       PLL, 6 (1970), 188-91.

A372   Rosenberg, Marvin. "On the Dating of Othello." ES,
       39 (1958), 72-4.
          Possibly Queen Anne's predilection for blacka-
       moors on the stage (as suggested by her express
       desire that actors with blackened skins appear in
       Jonson's Masque of Blackness) may have impelled
       Shakespeare to dramatize the story in Cinthio
       during the winter of 1604.

A373   Rosky, William. "Imagination in the English Renais-
       sance: Psychology and Poetic." SR, 5 (1958),
       49-73.
          Cites his examples from Jonson and others.

A374   Ross, Thomas W. "Expenses for Ben Jonson's The
       Masque of Beauty." BRMMLA, 23 (1969), 169-73.

A375   Rulfs, Donald J. "Reception of the Elizabethan Play-
       wrights on the London Stage, 1776-1883." SP, 46
       (1949), 54-69.
          Includes revivals and new editions of The Al-
       chemist, Volpone, Epicoene, and Every Man Out
       of His Humour.

A376   Sabol, Andrew J. "A Newly Discovered Contempo-
       rary Song Setting for Jonson's Cynthia's Revels."
       N&Q, N.S. 5 (1958), 384-5.

A377   _____. "Two Unpublished Stage Songs for the
       'Aery of Children.'" RN, 13 (1960), 222-31.
          Reproduces from MSS. the settings of "O the
       Ioyes that soone should waste" from Cynthia's

Revels (IV. iii), and "The darke is my delight"
from The Dutch Courtesan (I. ii); and discusses the
way in which the settings help to establish "some-
thing of the atmosphere of the earliest productions
of the choirboy plays. "

A378   Sackton, Alexander H.   "The Paradoxical Encomium
        in Elizabethan Drama. "   Texas Studies in Eng.,
        28 (1949), 83-104.
        The richest examples of the paradoxical ecomi-
        um are found in Ben Jonson, especially in Volpone.

A379   _____.   "The Rhymed Couplet in Ben Jonson's
        Plays. "   Texas Studies in Eng., 30 (1951), 86-106.

A380   Salingar, L. G.   "The Revenger's Tragedy: Some
        Possible Sources. "   MLR, 60 (1965), 3-12.
        Places the play with Volpone as works "based
        on a moral idea for which the dramatist invented
        a situation, filling it out with originally discon-
        nected items from his observation and reading. "

A381   _____.   "Farce and Fashion in The Silent Woman. "
        Essays and Studies, 20 (1967), 29-46.

A382   Savage, James E.   "Ben Jonson in Ben Jonson's
        Plays. "   UMSE, 3 (1962), 1-17.

A383   _____.   "The Cloaks of 'The Devil is an Asse.' "
        UMSE, 6 (1965), 5-14.

A384   _____.   "Some Antecedents of the Puppet Play in
        Bartholomew Fair. "   UMSE, 7 (1966), 42-64.

A385   _____.   "Ben Jonson and Shakespeare: 1623-
        1626. "   UMSE, 10 (1969), 25-48.
        The Staple of News as influenced by Timon,
        Julius Caesar, and Troilus.

A386   _____.   "The Formal Choruses in the Comedies
        of Ben Jonson. "   UMSE, 11 (1971), 11-21.

A387   Sawin, Lewis.   "The Earliest Use of 'Autumnal.' "
        MLN, 69 (1954), 558-9.
        Cites use of autumnal in the sense of "past the
        prime of Life" in Donne's Ninth Elegie, "The
        Autumnal, " and in Jonson's Epicoene I. i. 85.

A388   Scheve, D. A.   "Jonson's Volpone and Traditional
       Fox Love."   RES, N. S. 1 (1950), 242-4.
          Calls attention to a passage in Conrad Gesner's
       Historia Animalium (1557) which provides "the ani-
       mal structure" of the play; traces other occur-
       rences of the passage.

A389   Schlösser, A.   "Ben Jonson's Roman Plays."   Kwart-
       nalnik neofilologiczny (Warsaw), 8 (1961), 123-60.

A390   Scoufos, Alice Lyle.   "Nashe, Jonson, and the Old-
       castle Problem."   MP, 65 (1968), 307-24.
          What is mainly at issue here is the satiric
       treatment of Sir John Oldcastle (employed by Jon-
       son and Nashe to "needle" Eliza. Cobhams), and
       the reason Shakespeare was forced to change the
       name Oldcastle to Falstaff.

A391   Seronsy, Cecil C.   "A Skeltonic Passage in Ben Jon-
       son."   N&Q, 198 (1953), 24.
          Notes Iniquity's lines in Pug's cell at Newgate,
       The Devil is an Ass, V. vi. 25 ff.

A392   _____.   "Sir Politic Would-Be in Laputa."   ELN,
       1 (1963), 17-24.
          "In satirical matter portions of Swift's Gulliver's
       Travels bear extensive and suggestive resem-
       blances to Ben Jonson's Volpone."

A393   [no entry]

A394   Shaaber, M. A.   "The 'Vncleane Birds' in The Al-
       chemist."   MLN, 65 (1950), 106-9.
          Glosses IV. vii. 50-4 (Herford & Simpson) by a
       reference to birds with ruffs (1586) and the inter-
       pretation of the prodigy as a warning against pride.

A395   Shapiro, I. A.   "The 'Mermaid Club.'"   MLR, 45
       (1950), 6-17.
          Considers all the evidence about a "Mermaid
       Club" and its members; discusses the "Mitre
       feasters," the Sirenaics, and the verse letter to
       Jonson (if by Beaumont dated "most likely" 1613).

A396   Sharpe, Robert Boies.   "Jonson's 'Execration' and
       Chapman's 'Invective': Their Place in Their
       Author's Rivalry."   SP, 42 (1945), 555-63.

A397   Simonini, R. C., Jr. "Ben Jonson and John Florio."
        N&Q, 195 (1950), 512-13.
        Sees a reflection of Second Frutes in the last
        act of Eastward Ho!

A398   Simpson, Percy. "The Castle of the Rosy Cross:
        Ben Jonson and Theophilus Schweighardt." MLR,
        41 (1946), 206-7.
        Theophilus Schweighardt, Rosicrusian expositor,
        published in 1618 [Frankfurt a. M?] Speculum
        Sophicum Rhodo-Stauroticum. Das ist: weitläuffige
        Entdeckung dess Collegii und Axiomatum von derr
        ... Fraternitet Christ-Rosen-Creutz.

A399   _____. "A Modern Fable of Aesop." MLR, 43
        (1948), 403-5.
        Jonson's Poetaster, III. iv. 276-306. Aesop is
        Heminges, not Shakespeare; see H. D. Gray "The
        Chamberlain's Men and 'The Poetaster.'" MLR,
        42 (1947), 173-79.

A400   _____. "Francis Beaumont's Verse-Letter to Ben
        Jonson: 'The Sun, which doth the greatest com-
        fort bring....'" MLR, 46 (1951), 435-36.

A401   _____. "A Westminster Schoolboy and Ben Jon-
        son." TLS, Nov. 27, 1953, p. 761.
        Describes Gyles Oldisworth's "The Patterne of
        Pietye" (1638), a kind of Interlude mainly in prose
        with short verse passages which urges a proper
        tomb for Jonson in Westminster Abbey.

A402   Sirluck, Ernest. "Shakespeare and Jonson Among
        the Pamphleteers of the First Civil War: Some
        Unreported Seventeenth Century Allusions." MP,
        53 (1955), 88-99.

A403   Sisson, C. J. "Ben Jonson of Gresham College."
        TLS, Sept. 21, 1951, p. 604.
        Because Jonson identifies himself in a court
        suit involving the widow of Sir Walter Ralegh as
        "Benjamin Jonson of Gresham College in London,
        gent.," Sisson speculates that perhaps Jonson was
        a professor of rhetoric there during at least 1623.
        Being a professor would explain in part why Ox-
        ford gave him an M. A. in 1619. Perhaps Dis-
        coveries and the Grammar were originally written

as lecture notes for his classes. Cf. letter by
G. B. Johnston, TLS, Dec. 28, 1951, p. 837.
See Item No. 224.

A404   _____. "The Magic of Prospero." ShS, 2 (1958),
            70-77.
            Among other things, considers magic, alchemy,
            satire, and character in Jonson.

A405   Skelton, Robin. "The Masterpoet and the Multiple
            Tradition: The Poetry of Ben Jonson." Style, 1
            (1967), 225-46.

A406   Slights, William W. E.   "Epicoene and the Prose
            Paradox." PQ, 49 (1970), 178-87.
            "On the whole, Jonson seems to suffer his fools
            rather easily in Epicoene, allowing their preten-
            sions to social, sexual, and literary achievement
            to go largely unpunished. The discomfiture of
            Morose is typical in some ways of Jonson's di-
            minishing emphasis on punishment in the middle
            comedies. As moral attitudes become more close-
            ly integrated with artistic form in the plays, pun-
            ishment serves increasingly as emotional resolu-
            tion rather than as the execution of strict justice.
            Morose's folly is not of the sort that can be per-
            suasively dealt with by administering a stiff purge
            or prison sentence. Jonson chooses instead the
            indirect path to satire, the mock encomium and
            the paradoxical action of self-exposing folly. This
            is the method not only of the great comic artist
            but also of the serious, moral realist. In particu-
            lar, Jonson's moral realism is based on the as-
            sumption that the understanding of moral problems
            can be sharpened only through the proper mode of
            thinking about these problems. Paradox provided
            the dramatist just such a flexible way to present
            the serious themes of Epicoene" (p. 187).

A407   Sloan, Thomas O. "A Renaissance Controversialist on
            Rhetoric: Thomas Wright's Passions of the Mind
            in Generall." Speech Monographs, 36 (1969), 38-
            54.
            Considers the priest reputed to have converted
            Jonson.

A408   Snuggs, Henry L. "The Comic Humours: A New In-

terpretation. " <u>PMLA</u>, 62 (1947), 114-22.
The comic humors do not refer to human temperaments as defined by medical science of the
day but instead refer to the "pseudo-humours of
affectation and eccentricity. "

A409   . "The Source of Jonson's Definition of
Comedy. " <u>MLN</u>, 65 (1950), 543-4.
Finds Jonson's source of the Ciceronian defini-
tion (Every Man Out) in Minturno.

A410   Somerset, J. A. B. "William Poel's First Full Plat-
form Stage. " <u>Theatre Notebook</u>, 20.3 (1966), 118-
21.
Concerns the experiment undertaken for <u>When</u>
<u>You See Me, You Know Me</u>, <u>Sejanus</u>, and others.

A411   South, Malcolm H. "Animal Imagery in <u>Volpone</u>. "
<u>TSL</u>, 10 (1965), 141-50.

A412   Spanos, William V. "The Real Toad in the Jonsonian
Garden: Resonance in the Nondramatic Poetry. "
<u>JEGP</u>, 68 (1969), 1-23.
"A Jonsonian poem is indeed a highly wrought
artifact--the verbal equivalent of the formal sixteenth-century English garden--the linguistic texture of which is activated by what on the surface
appears to be an imperfection of one kind or other
in it. It is, as it were, jarred into motion, thus
rendering original what appears to be conventional,
spontaneous what appears to be imitative, subtle
what appears to be simple, and above all, alive
what appears to be inanimate" (p. 5).

A413   Sprague, Arthur Colby. "The Alchemist on the
Stage. " <u>Theatre Notebook</u>, 17 (1963), 46-7.

A414   Starnes, D. T. "The Figure Genius in the Renaissance. " <u>SR</u>, 11 (1964), 234-44.

A415   Starr, G. A. "Caesar's Just Cause. " <u>ShQ</u>, 17
(1966), 77-79.
Traces the line derisively quoted by Jonson,
"Caesar did never wrong, but with just cause, "
to Cicero's <u>De Officiis</u>.

A416   Steensma, Robert C. "Ben Jonson: A Checklist of

Editions, Biography, and Criticism, 1947-1964."
Research Opportunities in Renaissance Drama, 9
(1966), 29-46.

A417   Steese, Peter. "Jonson's A Song." Expli, 21.4
        (1962), Item 31.
            A note concerning "Oh do not wanton with those
        eyes."

A418   Stein, Arnold. "Plain Style, Plain Criticism, Plain
        Dealing, and Ben Jonson." ELH, 30 (1963), 306-
        16.
            A review essay of Wesley Trimpi's Ben Jonson's
        Poems: A Study of the Plain Style (Item No.
        B170 below). "To say that Jonson is one of the
        masters of plain style is not likely to provoke
        significant disagreement. The problems arise
        when the style is defined, when it is related to its
        past history and to its Renaissance development,
        and when Jonson's unquestionable mastery is des-
        cribed and explained by means of a severely
        limited set of terms" (p. 313).

A419   [no entry]

A420   Stevenson, Warren. "Shakespeare's Hand in The
        Spanish Tragedy 1602." SEL, 8 (1968), 307-21.
            Jonson's and Webster's styles are so unlike the
        Additions that we must look elsewhere.

A421   Stokes, E. E., Jr. "Jonson's 'Humour' Plays and
        Some Later Plays of Bernard Shaw." The
        Shavian, 2.10 (1964), 13-18.

A422   Stroud, Theodore A. "Ben Jonson and Father
        Thomas Wright." ELH, 14 (1947), 274-82.
            Offers some evidence that Wright was the
        Jesuit priest who converted Jonson to Catholicism
        when he was in prison in 1598.

A423   Summers, Joseph H. "The Heritage of Donne and
        Jonson." UTQ, 39 (1970), 107-26.
            "Donne and Jonson's inheritance was less im-
        portant as a fabulously rich collection of specific
        models than a suggestion of the possibilities avail-
        able for individual poets who were willing to ex-
        plore varying, and even contrasting, speakers,

genres, and literary ideals" (p. 126).

A424   Sylvester, William. "Jonson's 'Come, My Celia' and
        Catullus' 'Carmen V.'" Expl, 12.5 (1964), Item
        35.

A425   Tabachnich, Stephen E. "Jonson's Epitaph on Eliza-
        beth, L. H." Expl, 29 (1971), Item 77.
        Contends that between the lines Jonson is tell-
        ing us that Elizabeth died pregnant with an illegiti-
        mate child.

A426   Talbert, Ernest William. "The Purpose and Tech-
        nique of Jonson's Poetaster." SP, 42 (1945), 225-
        52.
        The play is "primarily a dramatic defense of
        poetry" and only incidentally personal satire.

A427   _____. "The Interpretation of Jonson's Courtly
        Spectacles." PMLA, 61 (1946), 454-73.
        Far from being flattery and pedantry, Jonson's
        masques are advice to the prince on the art of
        governing and recommendations of poetry to its
        natural protector, the court.

A428   _____. "Current Scholarly Works and the 'Erudi-
        tion' of Jonson's Masque of Augurs." SP, 44
        (1947), 605-24.
        Jonson used contemporary sources for classical
        references and brought classical learning into the
        court.

A429   Targan, Barry. "The Moral Structure of Bartholo-
        mew Fair." Discourse, 8 (1965), 276-84.
        "Bartholomew Fair, then, is a 'study' of hu-
        man frailty, which is a different thing than an at-
        tack upon it. And human frailty, the mature
        comic artist realizes, demands compassion--even
        if an ironic compassion--but not correction or
        scorn" (p. 279).

A430   Tave, Stuart M. "Corbyn Morris: Falstaff, Humor,
        and Comic Theory in the Eighteenth Century."
        MP, 50 (1952), 102-15.
        Contains discussion of Shakespearian and Jon-
        sonian comic characters.

A431   Taylor, Dick, Jr.   "The Masque and the Lance:
        The Third Earl of Pembroke in Jacobean Court
        Entertainments." Tulane Studies in English, 8
        (1958), 21-53.
            Discusses in some detail the Earl's relations
        with Jonson and Inigo Jones.

A432   Thayer, C. G.   "Ben Jonson, Markham, and Shakes-
        peare." N&Q, N. S. 1 (1954), 469-70.
            Suggests that Jonson, in following Markham's
        Cavelarice for his description of Win-the-Fight
        Littlewit in Bartholomew Fair, had also in mind
        the description of the horse in Venus and Adonis
        295-300, and may have intended to satirize Shakes-
        peare's stanza.

A433   _____. "Theme and Structure in The Alchemist."
        ELH, 26 (1959), 23-35.
            "The alchemical process involved is a progres-
        sive stripping away of the social veneer and a re-
        duction of the characters to representatives of the
        particular folly which is central to each of their
        motives" (p. 35).

A434   Thompson, W. L.   "The Source of the Flower Pas-
        sage in 'Lycidas.'" N&Q, 197 (1952), 97-9.
            Suggests that Milton was indebted to Jonson's
        Pan's Anniversary.

A435   Thomson, Patricia.   "The Literature of Patronage."
        EIC, 2 (1952), 267-84.
            Influence of patronage on Jonson and others.

A436   Thron, E. M.   "Jonson's Cynthia's Revels: Multi-
        plicity and Unity." SEL, 11 (1971), 235-47.
            "The display and unmasquing of vice for vir-
        tue's sake fulfills Criticus's purpose and unites
        the multiplicities of Cynthia's Revels: the cour-
        tiers will be mending their ways, Cupid is ban-
        ished, and the moral knowledge of Criticus re-
        ceives its proper reward from Cynthia" (p. 247).

A437   Townsend, Freda L.   "Ben Jonson's 'Censure' of
        Rutter's Shepheard's Holy-Day." MP, 44 (1947),
        238-47.
            Infers from Jonson's praise of Rutter's play
        and of Fletcher's Faithful Shepherdess and from

The Sad Shepherd that his "dramatic laws were
most probably original ... and had little to do with
ancient prescriptions."

A438   Trimpi, Wesley. "Jonson and the Neo-Latin Authori-
       ties for the Plain Style." PMLA, 77 (1962), 21-6.
       "Since he regarded the epistolary treatise as a gen-
       eral rhetorical statement, Jonson found ample contem-
       porary justification for using the plain style to treat
       any subject, either human or divine. The Renaissance
       treatises gave explicit rhetorical sanction to the prac-
       tice and stylistic assumptions of the ancient satirist,
       epigrammatist, and writer of comedy...." (p. 25).

A439   Ure, Peter. "Some Differences Between Senecan and
       Elizabethan Tragedy." Durham Univ. Journal,
       Dec. 1948, n.p.
       Belittles Senecan influence on Elizabethan tragedy
       in favor of 'romanitas, ' e.g. Chapman and Jonson.

A440   _____. "A simile in 'Samson Agonistes.'" N&Q,
       195 (1950), 298.
       Parallels to the woman-ship figure in Jonson's
       The Divelle is an Asse and The Staple of News.

A441   Van Deusen, Marshall. "Criticism and Ben Jonson's
       'To Celia.'" EIC, 7 (1957), 95-103.

A442   Velz, John W. "Clemency, Will, and Just Cause in
       'Julius Caesar.'" ShS, 22 (1969), 109-15.
       "If Shakespeare's Caesar did originally make a
       protestation about doing wrong only with just
       cause, he was, like Jonson, appealing to a view
       of clemency which can be found in De Clementia"
       (p. 115).

A443   Villiers, Jacob I. de. "Ben Jonson's Tragedies."
       ES, 45.6 (1964), 433-42.

A444   Waith, Eugene M. "The Poet's Morals in Jonson's
       Poetaster." MLQ, 12 (1951), 13-19.
       "Poetaster is a defense of poetry in which the
       social satire emphasized by Campbell [Comicall
       Satyre and Shakespeare's Troilus and Cressida] is
       an integral part, for the play presents the poet in
       his relations to society" (p. 19).

A445 _____ . "The Staging of Bartholomew Fair." SEL,
2.2 (1962), 181-95.
"If Bartholomew Fair was staged in the manner
I have described, it is one of the clearest examples
of the survival in the Elizabethan public theater of
the essentially medieval tradition of staging.
Though the 'special Decorum' of the Fair relates
the spectacle closely to Smithfield, the stage forms
are those of the old mansions and the conception
of space is that of the mysteries. Partly because
of this meeting of convention and realistic imitation,
the play also illustrates certain assumptions about
theatrical reality which underlie Elizabethan stage
craft. The illusion of Smithfield never obscures
the reality of the stage and frank admission of its
contrivances. The audience is often reminded that
it is witnessing a performance by the Lady Elizabeth's Men at the Hope Theater" (p. 194).

A446 _____ . "A Misprint in Bartholomew Fair." N&Q,
N.S. 10 (1963), 103-4.
V.v.50-1 (Herford and Simpson) should belong
to Grace Wellborn and not to Quarlous.

A447 Walker, Ralph S. "Literary Criticism in Jonson's
Conversations with Drummond." English, 8
(1951), 222-7.

A448 _____ . "Ben Jonson's Discoveries: A New New
Analysis." Essays and Studies, 5 (1952), 32-51.
Proposes to reduce the confusion of materials
in Discoveries as first and subsequently printed,
by arrangement in these categories: sententiae,
jottings, short essays, essay on statecraft, obser-
vations intended for teachers of the young, notes
(possibly for lectures), poetics.

A449 Warren, Michael J. "The Location of Jonson's
Catiline III, 490-754." PQ, 48 (1969), 561-65.
Argues for Lecca's house as The Location.

A450 Watson, Elizabeth. "Natural History in 'Love's
Martyr.'" Renaissance and Modern Studies (Univ.
of Nottingham), 8 (1964), 109-26.

A451 Watson, George. "Ramus, Miss Tuve, and the New
Petromachia." MP, 55 (1958), 259-62.

Rejects Tuve's linking of metaphysical style with
Ramism [in her Elizabethan and Metaphysical
Imagery, 1947] on the grounds that (1) the only
poets who are clearly Ramists--Sidney, Jonson,
and Milton--are not metaphysical, and (2) Ramism
was understood by English Renaissance poets as a
simplification (or even over-simplification) of logic
and hence would scarcely appeal to the metaphysi-
cals.

A452   Watson, Thomas L.   "The Detractor-Backbiter: Iago
        and the Tradition." TSLL, 5 (1964), 546-54.
        Considers Jonson's Every Man Out of His Hu-
        mour.

A453   Weld, John S.   "Christian Comedy: Volpone." SP,
        51 (1954), 172-93.
        "The folly here involved is the folly of worldli-
        ness and worldly wisdom, that paradoxical concept,
        developed by the church fathers, which became a
        favorite theme of late medieval and Renaissance
        satirists" (p. 173).

A453a   Wickham, Glynne.   "Contribution de Ben Jonson et
        de Dekker aux Fêtes du Couronnement de Jacques
        Ier." Fêtes de la Renaissance, 1957, pp. 279-83.

A454   Wiersma, Stanley M.   "Jonson's 'To John Donne.'"
        Expl, 25 (1966), Item 4.

A455   Williams, Raymond.   "Pastoral and Counter-Pastoral."
        Critical Quarterly, 10 (1968), 277-90.
        "And we can then remember that the whole re-
        sult of the fall from paradise was that instead of
        picking easily from an all-providing nature, man
        had to earn his bread in the sweat of his brow;
        that he incurred, as a common fate, the curse of
        labour. What really happens, in Jonson's and Ca-
        rew's celebrations of a rural order, is an extrac-
        tion of just this curse, by the power of art: a
        magical recreation of what can be seen as a natu-
        ral bounty and then a willing charity: each serving
        to ratify and bless the country landowner, or, by
        a characteristic reification, his house. Yet this
        extraction of the curse of labour is in fact achieved
        by a simple extraction of the existence of la-
        bourers" (p. 288).

A456   Wilson, Gayle Edward.   "Jonson's Use of the Bible
        and the Great Chain of Being in 'To Penshurst.'"
        SEL, 8 (1968), 77-89.
            "Jonson's statement on the proper way for man
        to live, then, is positive rather than negative.   To
        the comparison of the values manifested at Pens-
        hurst with those advocated by ancient authors (the
        humanistic-classical approach to the problem),
        Jonson, as the priest-poet, adds the dimension of
        biblical values as they were interpreted in the
        seventeenth century.   Fulfilling this role, he des-
        cribes Penshurst in these terms, thus creating his
        'fable', and contrasts it with estates that fail to
        embody these principles.   By this means, he
        counsels the Sidneys, and by extension all men,
        on the proper way in which to govern their land,
        be it an estate or kingdom.   They must imitate in
        small the divine law, manifested by the Great
        Chain of Being, that governs the universe.   The
        only way in which man can achieve this end, Jon-
        son makes clear, is to practice the ethical stan-
        dards based on the religious 'Truth' contained in
        the Old and New Testaments" (pp. 88-89).

A457   Wilson, J. Dover.   "Ben Jonson and Julius Caesar."
        ShS, 2 (1949), 36-43.
            Finds echoes in Jonson's plays of Julius Caesar,
        argues that the well-known criticism in Discoveries
        refers to words of Caesar still heard in perform-
        ances based on the prompt-book for at least three
        years after the appearance of the Folio version,
        and discusses problems involved in the Folio
        "change."

A458   _____ .   "Shakespeare's 'Small Latin'--How Much?"
        ShS, 10 (1957), 12-26.
            Attempts to arbitrate between adherents of Ben
        Jonson's view and the "claims in favor of Shakes-
        peare's learning advanced by learned men who de-
        sire to have him of their company."

A459   Winzeler, Charlotte.   "Curse upon a God: Classical
        and Elizabethan Thought Blended."   Brigham
        Young University Studies, 5 (1964),   87-94.
            "The basic skeleton of 'An Execration upon Vul-
        can' is a prayer form of the Elizabethan Anglican
        Church, to which Jonson belonged" (p. 90).

A460   Withington, Eleanor. "Nicholas Briot and Jonson's
        Commendation of Joseph Rutter." N&Q, 198
        (1953), 152-3.
            Jonson's commendatory lines to the Shepherd's
        Holy-Day (1635) refers to Briot's new method of
        coinage as a reminder to Rutter to make nice dis-
        tinctions among the levels of language as required
        by the decorum of character; but Rutter, who mis-
        interpreted the advice as favoring uniformity in all
        poetry, may have been encouraged to support a
        standard foreshadowing the critical principles of
        the Augustan Age.

A461   Woods, Charles B. and Curt A. Zimansky, eds.
        Studies in English Drama. Presented to Baldwin
        Maxwell, Editor of PQ, 1929-1955. PQ, 41.1
        (Jan. 1962), Iowa City: State Univ. Iowa.
            Includes F. L. Huntley, "Ben Jonson and An-
        thony Munday, The Case is Altered Altered Again,"
        pp. 205-214, and R. Putney, "Jonson's Poetic
        Comedy," pp. 188-204.
            Reviewed: H. W. Donner, Studia Neophilologica,
        34 (1962), 340-1; TLS, July 27, 1962, p. 542;
        Hermann Heuer, SJ, 98 (1962), 295-7.

A462   Wren, Robert M. "Ben Jonson as Producer." ETJ,
        22 (1970), 284-90.

A463   Wronker, Stanley S. "Pope and Ben Jonson." N&Q,
        196 (1951), 495-6.
            Sees a "more than superficial" parallel between
        Pope's description of man in Essay On Man, II,
        18, and Jonson's characterization of Shakespeare.

A464   Wykes, David. "Ben Jonson's 'Chast Booke': The
        Epigrammes." Renaissance and Modern Studies
        (Univ. of Nottingham), 13 (1969), 76-87.
            "Many of the Epigrammes are satirical and
        those of approbation cannot be divorced from the
        reformer's zeal. To do so is largely to miss
        their point. Jonson may not be a zealot, but
        here, as almost everywhere else, he is concerned
        with morals and society. The eulogies among the
        Epigrammes are relevant to this concern in that
        they are exemplary poems. The persons praised
        are meant to act for the reader as moral exem-
        plars. Blame and praise are two sides of the

same coin" (pp. 76-77).

A465   Zwicker, Steven N. "Dryden's Borrowing from Ben
       Jonson's 'Panegyre.'" N&Q, 213 (1968), 105-6.
       "Prologue to John Banks' The Unhappy Favorite
       used line 162 of 'Panegyre.'"

BOOKS AND MONOGRAPHS

B1 Asthana, R. K. "The Dynamics of Jonson's Come-
    dies," Criticism and Research. Banaras Hindu
    Univ., 1964, pp. 46-55.

B2 Atkins, J. W. H. English Literary Criticism: The
    Renascence. London: Methuen, 1947.
    Includes an account of Jonson's critical writings.

B3 Babb, Lawrence. The Elizabethan Malady. A Study
    of Melancholia in English Literature from 1580-1642.
    Lansing: Michigan State College Press, 1951.

B4 Baldini, Gabriele, ed. La fortuna di Shakespeare
    (1593-1964). 2 Vols. Milan: Casa editrice Il Sag-
    giatore, 1965.
    An Italian translation of Jonson's commendatory
    verses for The Shakespeare Folio is included.

B5 Bamborough, J. B. Ben Jonson. Writers and Their
    Work, No. 112. London, New York: Longmans,
    Green, 1959; collected in British Writers and Their
    Work, No. 11. Lincoln: Nebraska Univ. Press,
    1966.
    Stresses that Jonson was both classical and ro-
    mantic, deliberately combining the best of both tra-
    ditions.

B6 _____. Ben Jonson. London: Hutchinson, 1970.

B7 Barber, C. L. The Idea of Honour in the English
    Drama, 1591-1700. Gothenburg Studies in English,
    VI. Göteborg: Elanders Boktryckeri Aktiebolag,
    1957.
    This study (originally a dissertation at Univ. of
    Gothenburg) presents a discussion of honor in Jon-

95

son's major plays.

B8　Barish, Jonas A.　Ben Jonson and the Language of
　　　Prose Comedy.　Cambridge, Mass.:　Harvard Univ.
　　　Press, 1960.
　　　Reviewed:　SCN, 18 (1960), Nos. 2-3, 30 (item
　　　31); J. A. Bryant, Jr., MLQ, 21 (1960), 372-3; R.
　　　Davril, Etudes Anglaises, 14 (1961), 243-4; Peter
　　　Ure, N&Q, N.S. 8 (1961), 196-8; S. E. Sprott,
　　　Dalhousie Rev., 41 (1961), 88-91; Wm. Blissett,
　　　UTQ, 30 (1961), 251-4; H. C. Heffner, QJS, 47
　　　(1961), 74-81; Milton Crane, SQ, 12 (1961), 336-8;
　　　Ed. Partridge, JEGP, 41 (1962), 399-402; C. G.
　　　Thayer, BA, 36 (1962), 72; G. K. Hunter, RES, 13
　　　(1962), 193-6; E. G. Fogel, RN, 15 (1962), 42-5.

B9　＿＿＿＿＿, ed. Ben Jonson. A Collection of Critical
　　　Essays.　Englewood Cliffs, N. J.:　Prentice-Hall,
　　　1963.
　　　Essays previously published.
　　　Reviewed:　Hugh Maclean, UTQ, 33 (1963), 89-97.

B10　＿＿＿＿＿, ed.　Jonson:　'Volpone'; a Casebook.　Lon-
　　　don:　Macmillan, 1972.

B11　Baum, Helena Watts.　The Satiric and The Didactic in
　　　Ben Jonson's Comedies.　Chapel Hill:　Univ. of
　　　North Carolina Press, 1947.
　　　Reviewed:　G. B. Johnston, South Atlantic Bull.,
　　　14 (1948), 1, 13-4; G. B. Evans, JEGP, 47 (1948),
　　　306-8; F. R. Johnson, MLN, 64 (1949), 213; A.
　　　Davenport, MLR, 44 (1949), 402-3.

B12　Bentley, Gerald Eades.　Shakespeare and Jonson.
　　　Their Reputations in the Seventeenth Century Com-
　　　pared.　2 Vols. Chicago:　Univ. of Chicago Press,
　　　1945.
　　　Reviewed:　TLS, April 28, 1945, p. 200; N&Q,
　　　188 (1945), 241-2; Alfred Harbage, MLN, 60 (1945),
　　　414-7; Baldwin Maxwell, PQ, 24 (1945), 91-3;
　　　Pierce Butler, Lib. Quar., 15 (1945), 268-9; Per-
　　　cy Simpson, RES, 21 (1945), 334-6; Theatre Arts,
　　　29 (1945), 254-5; C. J. Sisson, MLR, 41 (1946),
　　　73-4; T. W. Baldwin, JEGP, 45 (1946), 232-4; F.
　　　P. Wilson, Library, 4th S, 1946, 26, 199-202; R.
　　　S. Knox, UTQ, 17 (1947), 100-1.

B13 _____ . The Swan of Avon and the Bricklayer of
Westminster. Inaugural lecture in Princeton Univ.,
March 15, 1946. Princeton: Princeton Univ. Press,
1948.

B14 _____ , ed. The Seventeenth-Century Stage: A Collection of Critical Essays. Chicago: Chicago Univ.
Press, 1968.
    One of these is Jonson's Introduction to Bartholo-
mew Fair.

B15 Berlin, Normand. The Base String: The Underworld
in Elizabethan Drama. Rutherford, N.J.: Fairleigh
Dickinson Univ. Press, 1968.
    Chapter 4 of this study deals with Jonson and his
treatment of that variety of Thieves, Rogues, and
Vagabonds that populate the "Elizabethan underworld." The title of the book derives from Prince
Hal, who asserts (in 1H4) that he has "sounded the
very base-string of humility," commenting upon his
relationship to lower elements of society. The Alchemist, Bartholomew Fair, and The Devil is an
Asse are treated in special detail. Concludes that
the underworld of Jonson's plays is not "a hateful
world preying upon honest citizens, as it often is in
Dekker's plays," but, rather, "a neutral world--and
in Bartholomew Fair a warmly human world--prey-
ing upon fools" (p. 171).

B15a Bevington, David. "Shakespeare vs. Jonson on Satire,"
in Shakespeare 1971: Proceedings of the World
Shakespeare Congress, Vancouver, August 1971, ed.
Clifford Leech and J. M. R. Margeson. Toronto:
Univ. of Toronto Press, 1972, pp. 107-122.

B16 Black, Matthew. "Enter Citizens" in Studies in English Renaissance Drama, ed. J. W. Bennett, O.
Carghill, V. Hall, Jr. New York: New York Univ.
Press, 1959.
    Discusses the place of minor figures in Shakes-
peare, Marlowe, Kyd, Jonson, and others.

B17 Blanchard, R. A. "Thomas Carew and the Cavalier
Poets," Transactions of Wisconsin Academy, 43
(1954), n.p.
    The influence of Donne upon Carew is modified
by Jonson.

B17a Bluestone, Max and Norman Rabkin, eds. Shakes-
      peare's Contemporaries. Englewood Cliffs, N.J.:
      Prentice-Hall, Inc., 1961.
          Includes: Henry L. Snuggs, "The Comic Hu-
      mours: A New Interpretation" [A408]; Jonas A.
      Barish, "The Double Plot in Volpone" [A19]; C. H.
      Herford and Percy Simpson, "The Alchemist"; and
      Ray L. Heffner, Jr., "Unifying Symbols in the
      Comedy of Ben Jonson" [A195].

B18   Boas, Frederick S. An Introduction to Stuart Drama.
      Oxford: Oxford University Press, 1946.
          Comments on individual dramatists, including
      Jonson.

B19   Boughner, Daniel C. The Braggart in Renaissance
      Comedy. Minneapolis: Univ. of Minnesota Press,
      1954; London: Oxford Univ. Press, 1954.
          "... in a line of development that leads from
      Mankind in The Castle of Perseverance ... to Jon-
      son's Fastidious Brisk."

B20   _____. The Devil's Disciple: Ben Jonson's Debt
      to Machiavelli. New York: Philosophical Library,
      1968.

B21   Bradbrook, M. C. The Growth and Structure of
      Elizabethan Comedy. London: Chatto and Windus,
      1955.
          The purpose is "to trace the evolution and the
      interaction" of the two comic forms which culminate
      in Shakespeare and Jonson respectively.

B22   Brooks, Cleanth, and William K. Wimsatt. "English
      Neo-Classicism: Dryden and Jonson," in Literary
      Criticism: A Short History. New York: Random
      House, 1957, pp. 174-95.

B23   Brown, Huntington. Rabelais in English Literature.
      Cambridge, Mass.: Harvard Univ. Press, 1933;
      reissued by Frank Cass, 1967.
          Demonstrates the presence of Rabelais in a
      masque by Ben Jonson.

B24   Bryant, J. A., Jr. "A Tale of A Tub: Jonson's
      Comedy of the Human Condition." Renaissance
      Papers 1963. Durham, N.C.: Southeastern

Renaissance Conf., 95-105.

B25 Bush, Douglas. English Literature in the Earlier
     Seventeenth Century, 1600-1660. Oxford: Clarendon
     Press, 1945.
     Contains an extensive chapter on "Jonson, Donne
     and Their Successors."

B26 Capone, Giovanna. Ben Jonson: L'iconologia verbale
     come strategia de commedia. Bologna: Casa Edi-
     trice Patron, 1969.

B27 Castle, Edward J. Shakespeare, Bacon, Jonson, and
     Greene: A Study. Port Washington, New York:
     Kennikat, 1970.
     Reprint of 1897 ed.

B28 Champion, Larry S. Ben Jonson's "Dotages": A Re-
     consideration of the Late Plays. Lexington: Univ.
     of Kentucky Press, 1967.
     Reviewed: C. G. Thayer, Ren. Q., 21 (1968),
     363-5.

B29 Chute, Marchette. Ben Jonson of Westminster. New
     York: E. P. Dutton & Co., 1953.
     Reviewed: Alfred Harbage, N. Y. Times Book
     Rev., Oct. 18, 1953, pp. 3-38; Joseph Wood
     Krutch, Sat. Rev. Lit., Oct. 17, 1953, pp. 13-4;
     Samuel C. Chew, N. Y. Herald Tribune Book Rev.,
     Oct. 18, 1953, pp. 1-13; Charles Tyler Prouty,
     Yale Review, 43 (1954), pp. 471-3; Nation, Jan. 9,
     1954, p. 37 [brief]; Hermann Heuer, SJ, 91 (1955),
     317-8; M. Poirier, Etudes Anglaises, 8 (1955), 339-
     40.

B30 Cook, Elizabeth. "More Books," The Bulletin of the
     Boston Public Library, 6th series, Vol. 22 (October
     1947).
     Article concerns Richard Brome's plays; stresses
     the fact that though Jonson was his master, "he
     learned the craft not from Jonson's principles but
     his practice."

B31 Cunningham, J. E. Elizabethan and Early Stuart
     Drama. Literature in Perspective. New York:
     Evans Bros., 1965 [Paper].
     Concentrates on Marlowe, Jonson, and Massinger.

B32 Curry, John V., S.J. Deception in Elizabethan Come-
     dy. Chicago: Loyola Univ. Press, 1955.
     EMO is discussed in Chapter 2 ("Deception and
     Its Agents"), Volpone in Chapter 7 ("The Audience
     Appeal of Deception").

B33 Davis, Joe Lee. The Sons of Ben. Jonsonian Comedy
     in Caroline England. Detroit: Wayne State Univ.
     Press, 1967.
     Reviewed: Jonas A. Barish, MLQ, 29 (1968),
     356-8.

B34 DeLuna, Barbara Nielson. Jonson's Romish Plot: A
     Study of 'Catiline' and Its Historical Context. Ox-
     ford: Clarendon Press, 1967.
     Reviewed: S. Warhaft, Dal. Rev., 47 (1967),
     413-16; Edward Partridge, Ren. Q., 21 (1968), 232-
     36; Peter Ure, N&Q, 213 (1968), 274-76.

B35 Demaray, John G. Milton and the Masque Tradition:
     The Early Poems, Arcades and Comus. Cambridge,
     Mass.: Harvard Univ. Press, 1968; Oxford: Ox-
     ford Univ. Press, 1968.
     Using Jonsonian criteria, discusses Milton's
     masque in terms of the tradition.

B36 Dessen, Alan C. Jonson's Moral Comedy. Evanston:
     Northwestern Univ. Press, 1971.

B36a deVocht, Henry. Comments on the Text of Ben Jon-
     son's Cynthias Revels; An Investigation into the
     Comparative Value of the 1601-Quarto and 1616-
     Folio. Materials for the Study of the Old English
     Drama, N. S. V. 21. Louvain: Uystpruyst, 1950.

B36b _____. Studies on the Texts of Ben Jonson's
     Poetaster and Sejanus. Materials for the Study of
     Old English Drama, N. S., V. 27. Louvain:
     Uystpruyst, 1958.

B37 Dobbs, Leonard. Shakespeare Revealed. Skeffington,
     England, 1951.
     Reconstructed life of Shakespeare, with Jonson
     ·as Falstaff.

B38 Donaldson, Ian. The World Upside-Down: Comedy
     from Jonson to Fielding. London: Oxford Univ.

Press, 1970.
Of particular interest are chapters 2 ("'A Martyr's Resolution': Epicoene") and 3 ("'Days of Privilege': Bartholomew Fair").

B39 Doolittle, Hilda. By Avon River. New York: Macmillan, 1949.
Prose and verse historical/imaginary pictures of Shakespeare and contemporaries, including Jonson.

B40 Doran, Madeleine. Endeavors of Art: A Study of Form in Elizabethan Drama. Madison: Univ. of Wisconsin Press, 1954.
Jonson and his works are discussed passim., while chapter 7 draws comparisons between Jonsonian and Shakespearian comedy.

B41 Dunn, Esther C. Ben Jonson's Art: Elizabethan Life and Literature as Reflected Therein. New York: Russell and Russell, 1963.
Reprint of 1925 ed.

B42 Enck, John J. Jonson and the Comic Truth. Madison: Univ. of Wisconsin Press, 1957.
"The comic truth must have such qualities: follies based on contemporary foibles, characters reduced to simplified drives, a neatly turned conclusion and clarity throughout" (p. 247).
Reviewed: Edward Partridge, MP, 56 (1958), 133-5; SCN, 16 (1958), 10; Marvin T. Herrick, JEGP, 57 (1958), 547-9; C. G. Thayer, BA, 32 (1958), 444; N&Q, N.S. 5 (1958), 494-5; J. B. Bamborough, RES, 10 (1959), 306-8; Jackson I. Cope, MLN, 74 (1959), 738-41; Lisle C. John, CE, 20 (1959), 326-7; J. A. Bryant, Jr., Sewanee Rev., 67 (1959), 699-700.

B43 Enright, D. J. "Poetic Satire and Satire in Verse." The Apothecary's Shop. London: Secker and Warburg, 1957, pp. 54-74.
See A136 for annotation.

B44 Evans, Maurice. English Poetry in the Sixteenth Century. Univ. Library Series. London: Hutchinson & Co., 1955.
Jonson is mentioned often but is not treated in a sustained effort.

B45   Fieler, Frank B. "The Impact of Bacon and the New
       Science Upon Jonson's Critical Thought in Timber, "
       in Renaissance Papers 1958, 1959, 1960. Durham,
       N. C.: Southeast Ren. Conf., 84-92.
          Jonson's "break with the sixteenth century's fol-
       lowing of classical authority is intimately connected
       with the general break with the past proclaimed by
       Francis Bacon in the Advancement of Learning. It
       seems highly probable because of their close simi-
       larity that Jonson's critical method in Timber was
       indebted to those methods Bacon championed for the
       true transmission of knowledge in the Advancement
       of Learning. " (See especially pp. 91-92)

B46   Fraser, P. M., ed. The Wares of Autolycus: Se-
       lected Literary Essays of Alice Meynell. Oxford:
       Oxford Univ. Press, 1965.
          Discussions of Jonson, Marvell, and others.

B47   Fricker, Franz. Ben Jonson's Plays in Performance
       and The Jacobean Theatre. Bern: Krande, 1972.

B48   Friedman, William F. and Elizabeth S. Friedman.
       The Shakespearean Ciphers Examined: An Analysis
       of Cryptographic Systems Used as Evidence that
       Someone Other than William Shakespeare Wrote the
       Plays Commonly Attributed to Him. Cambridge:
       Cambridge U. Press, 1957.
          Examines closely the methods of Elizabeth Wells
       Gallup, who listed Shakespeare, Jonson, and others
       as masks for Bacon.

B49   Friedson, Anthony M. Literature through the Ages.
       New York: Oak Tree Press, 1964.
          Very brief consideration of The Silent Woman.

B50   Furniss, W. Todd. "Ben Jonson's Masques, " in Three
       Studies in the Renaissance: Sidney, Jonson, Milton,
       ed. B. C. Nangle. New Haven: Yale Univ. Press,
       1958, pp. 89-179.
          Reviewed: SCN, 16 (1958), 40 [brief]; Irving Rib-
       ner, MLN, 74 (1959), 162-4; Michel Poirier, Etudes
       Anglaises, 12 (1959), 351; M. C. Bradbrook, MLR,
       54 (1959), 584-5; John Buxton, RES, 11 (1960), 202-
       3.

B51   Frye, Northrop. Anatomy of Criticism: Four Essays.
      Princeton: Princeton Univ. Press, 1957.
         Jonson's work is discussed by means of example
      in The Third Essay, and elsewhere.

B52   _____. A Natural Perspective: The Development
      of Shakespearean Comedy and Romance. New York:
      Harcourt, Brace & World, 1965.
         "The contrast between Shakespeare and Ben Jon-
      son is hackneyed, but, like many hackneyed sub-
      jects, not exhausted" (p. 14). The title of chapter
      1--"Mouldy Tales"--derives from Jonson's scolding
      the public for preferring "some mouldy tale like
      Pericles" to The New Inn. The discussion of Jon-
      son's play in comparison to Shakespeare that follows
      is central to the chapter.

B53   Gagen, Jean. The New Woman: Her Emergence in
      English Drama 1600-1730. New York: Twayne Pub-
      lishers, 1954.
         Among the examples cited is Lady Would-Be in
      Volpone.

B54   Gardner, Thomas. "'A Parodie! A Parodie!'" in
      Lebende Antike: Sumposion für Rudolf Sühnel, ed.
      Meller, Horst and Hans-Joachim Zimmermann.
      Berlin: E. Schmidt, 1967, pp. 197-206.

B55   Gibbons, Brian. Jacobean City Comedy: A Study of
      Satiric Plays by Jonson, Marston, and Middleton.
      Cambridge, Mass.: Harvard Univ. Press, 1968;
      London: Hart-Davis, 1968.

B56   Gilbert, Allan H. The Symbolic Persons in the Masques
      of Ben Jonson. Durham, N.C.: Duke University
      Press, 1948.
         A dictionary.
         Reviewed: J. H. McDowell, JEGP, 48 (1949),
      412-13; D. E. Baughan, South Atlantic Bull., 14
      (1949), 4, 5; H. W. Wells, Shakespeare Assoc.
      Bull., 24 (1949), 237-8; N&Q, 194 (1949), 373; S.
      C. Chew, MLN, 45 (1950), 136-38; M. Praz, Itali-
      ca, 27 (1950), 348-9; P. Simpson, MLR, 45 (1950),
      241-3.

B57   _____, ed. Renaissance Papers. A selection of
      papers presented at the Ranaissance Meeting in the

Southeastern States, Duke Univ., April 12-13, 1957.
Southeastern Renaissance Conference.
Includes Cyrus Hoy, "The Pretended Piety of
Jonson's Alchemist, " pp. 15-19; see B74.
Reviewed: RN, 10 (1957), 105-6; Glenn H. Blay-
ney, SQ, 9 (1958), 76-7.

B58   Goodman, Paul. "Comic Plots: The Alchemist, " in
The Structure of Literature. Chicago: Univ. of
Chicago Press, 1954, pp. 82-103.

B59   Gottwald, Maria. Satirical Elements in Ben Jonson's
Comedy. Travaux de la Société des Sciences et
des Lettres de Wroclaw. Wroclaw, 1969.
Begins with a discussion of Jonson's relationship
to "The Renaissance notion of satire. " YWES described her later chapters on the individual plays
as "sensible and well-ordered accounts, " singling
out the treatments of Epicoene and Bartholomew
Fair for particular praise.

B60   Greg, W. W. A Bibliography of the English Printed
Drama to the Restoration. Vol. III: Collections,
Appendix, Reference Lists: 24 Plates. Oxford:
Oxford Univ. Press. For The Bibliographical Society,
1957.
Included and described are the folio collections
of Shakespeare and Jonson.

B61   _____. "The Riddle of Jonson's Chronology, " in
The Collected Papers of Sir Walter W. Greg, ed.
J. C. Maxwell. Oxford: Clarendon Press, 1966,
pp. 184-91.
Reprint of an important article first published in
The Library (March 1926).

B62   _____. "Was There a 1612 Quarto of Epicoene?"
in The Collected Papers of Sir Walter W. Greg,
ed. J. C. Maxwell. Oxford: Clarendon Press,
1966, pp. 314-21.
Reprint of an essay that first appeared in The
Library 15 (Dec. 1934), 306-15.

B63   Gum, Colburn. The Aristophanic Comedies of Ben
Jonson: A Comparative Study of Jonson and Aristophanes. The Hague: Mouton, 1969.

B64 Halliday, F. E. The Cult of Shakespeare. London:
Duckworth, 1957.
Shakespeare's popularity was eclipsed in the gene-
rations after his death by that of Beaumont and
Fletcher and Jonson.

B65 Hardison, O. B., Jr. The Enduring Monument: A
Study of The Idea of Praise in Renaissance Literary
Theory and Practice. Chapel Hill: Univ. of No.
Carolina Press, 1962.
A number of Jonson's poems are treated in the
course of this study.

B66 Heffner, Ray L., Jr. "Unifying Symbols in The Come-
dy of Ben Jonson, " in Elizabethan Drama: Modern
Essays in Criticism, ed. R. J. Kaufman. New
York: Oxford (Galaxy), 1961.

B67 Hemphill, George, ed. Discussions of Poetry: Rhythm
and Sound. Boston: D. C. Heath, 1961.
Observes that Jonson was among poets concerned
with a theory of appropriate sound effects in poetry.

B68 Heninger, S. K., Jr. A Handbook of Renaissance
Meteorology. Durham, N.C.: Duke Univ. Press,
1960; Cambridge: Cambridge Univ. Press, 1960.
Part III considers Spenser and Jonson "in the
light of Renaissance meteorology. "

B69 Herrick, Marvin T. Tragicomedy: Its Origin and De-
velopment in Italy, France, & England. Urbana:
Univ. of Illinois Press, 1962.
Brief discussions of Jonson throughout.

B70 Holden, William P. Anti-Puritan Satire, 1572-1642.
New Haven: Yale Univ. Press; Oxford: Oxford
Univ. Press, 1954.
Contains section dealing with Puritans in Shake-
speare, Middleton, and, especially, Jonson.

B71 Holzknecht, Karl J. Outlines of Tudor and Stuart
Plays, 1497-1642. London: Methuen & Co., Ltd.,
1947.
Contains a section on Ben Jonson (pp. 168-216)
that includes a biographical statement, and outlines
of the following plays: Every Man in His Humor,
Sejanus, his Fall, Volpone, or the Fox, Epicoene,

The Alchemist, Bartholomew Fair, and The Staple
of News.

B72   Howarth, Herbert. "The Joycean Comedy: Wilde,
      Jonson, and Others." James Joyce Miscellany,
      Second Series, ed. Marvin Magalaner. Carbondale:
      Southern Illinois Univ. Press, 1959, pp. 179-94.

B73   Howarth, R. G. A Pot of Gillyflowers: Studies and
      Notes. Cape Town: Privately printed, 1965 (cyclo-
      styled).
      Short studies or notes on Jonson.

B74   Hoy, Cyrus. "The Pretended Piety of Jonson's Al-
      chemist," Renaissance Papers. Durham, N. C. :
      Southeastern Renaissance Conference, 1958, pp. 15-
      19.

B75   Hyde, Mary Crapo. Playwriting for Elizabethans,
      1600-1605. New York: Columbia Univ. Press and
      Oxford Univ. Press, 1949.
      From a detailed examination of dramas by Shake-
      speare, Jonson, and others, she attempts to deter-
      mine what these authors and their audiences looked
      for in structure, theme, and characterization.

B76   Inglis, Fred. The Elizabethan Poets: The Making of
      English Poetry from Wyatt to Ben Jonson. London:
      Evans Brothers, Ltd., 1969, pp. 127-56.
      Emphasizes the virtues of poets writing in the
      plain style. Contains a chapter entitled "Jonson the
      Master: Stones Well Squared. "

B77   Jackson, Gabriele B. Vision and Judgment in Ben Jon-
      son's Drama. New Haven: Yale Univ. Press, 1968.

B78   Jayne, Sears. Library Catalogues of the English
      Ranaissance. Berkeley: California Univ. Press and
      Cambridge Univ. Press, 1957.
      Among the private libraries catalogued is Jonson's.

B79   Johansson, Bertil. Religion and Superstition in the
      Plays of Ben Jonson and Thomas Middleton. Essays
      and Studies on English Language and Literature, 7.
      Upsala: A. -B. Lundequistska Bokhandeln, 1950;
      Cambridge, Mass.: Harvard Univ. Press, 1950.

B80 _____. Law and Lawyers in Elizabethan England,
as Evidenced in the Plays of Ben Jonson and Thomas
Middleton. Stockholm Studies in English, 18.
Stockholm: Almqvist and Wiksell, 1967.

B81 Johnson, Carol Holmes. Reason's Double Agents.
Chapel Hill: Univ. of North Carolina Press, 1966.
Reason in Donne, Jonson, Pope, Tate, Winters,
and Berryman.

B82 Johnston, George Burke. Ben Jonson: Poet. Columbia Univ. Studies in English and Comparative Literature, No. 162. New York: Columbia Univ. Press,
1945.
"Without avoiding mention of masques and plays,
this study is to deal primarily with the non-dramatic
poems. It is not concerned so much with the 'goodness' or 'badness' of the works, but rather with an
attempt to find out what kind of poet Jonson is,
what his conception of poetry was, what materials
he used (that is, what he considered poetic), and
if possible why he was a poet" (p. 4).
Reviewed: E. W. Talbert, MLN, 61 (1946),
205-7; A. M., KR, 8 (1946), 170-1.

B83 Jones-Davies, M. Thomas. Inigo Jones, Ben Jonson
et le Masque. Paris: Didier, 1967.
Reviewed: Michel Grivelet, Etudes Anglaises,
21 (1968), 198-99.

B84 Jungnell, T. "Notes on the Language of Ben Jonson, "
Studier i Modern Språkvetenskap, n. d., n. p., n. pag.
Collection of grammatical phenomena found in the
Folio (1616) edition of Jonson's works.

B85 Kaufmann, R. J., ed. Elizabethan Drama: Modern
Essays in Criticism. Galaxy Books, 63. New
York: Oxford Univ. Press, 1961.
Contains L. C. Knights, "Tradition and Ben Jon-
son"; Ray L. Heffner, Jr., "Unifying Symbols in
the Comedy of Ben Jonson, " and Robert Ornstein,
"The Moral Vision of Ben Jonson's Tragedy. "

B86 Keast, William R., ed. Seventeenth-Century English
Poetry: Modern Essays in Criticism. New York:
Oxford Univ. Press, 1962.
Includes Geoffrey Walton's "The Tone of Ben

Jonson's Poetry, " pp. 193-214; see B174 for annotation.

B87   Kernan, Alvin B.   The Cankered Muse: Satire of the
       English Renaissance.   New Haven: Yale Univ.
       Press, 1959.
       Discussion of Jonson and most of his major plays
       throughout.

B88   _____. The Plot of Satire.   New Haven: Yale
       Univ. Press, 1965.
       General comments on Jonson throughout.   Chap-
       ter 9 is devoted to an extensive analysis of Volpone:
       "In short, Jonson attacked the new dream of man
       that he was free to make himself and his world
       over, in the image of his desires, rather than work-
       ing slowly and patiently with a stubborn Nature"
       (p. 121).

B88a   Kirsch, Arthur A.   "Guarini and Jonson, " Jacobean
       Dramatic Perspectives.   Charlottesville: Univ. of
       Virginia Press, 1972, pp. 7-24.

B89   Kirschbaum, Leo.   "Jonson, Seneca, and Mortimer, "
       in Studies in Honor of John Wilcox, ed. A. Dayle
       Wallace and Woodburn O. Ross.   Detroit: Wayne
       State Univ. Press, 1958, pp. 9-22.

B90   Klein, David.   The Elizabethan Dramatists as Critics.
       New York: Philosophical Lib., 1963.
       Reviewed: T. W. Baldwin, JEGP, 64 (1965),
       293-4; Pierre Legouis, Etudes Anglaises, 19 (1966),
       182-3.

B91   Knights, L. C.   "Ben Jonson, Dramatist, " in Guide
       to Eng. Lit., Vol. II, ed. Boris Ford.   Baltimore:
       Penguin Books, 1956, pp. 302-11.

B92   _____. Drama and Society in the Age of Jonson.
       Penguin Books.   London: Chatto and Windus, 1962.
       Reissue of work first published in 1937.
       Reviewed: R. Davril, Etudes Anglaises, 16
       (1963), pp. 182-3.

B93   Knoll, Robert E.   Ben Jonson's Plays: An Introduc-
       tion.   Lincoln: Univ. of Nebraska Press, 1964.
       The most successful of Jonson's plays derive

primarily from indigenous rather than classical
sources.
Reviewed: C. J. Gianakaris, JEGP, 64 (1965),
727-30; F. S. K., Personalist, 50 (1965), 558-9;
Richard W. Van Fossen, SAQ, 64 (1965), 575; Norman N. Holland, RN, 18 (1965), 345-6; David Novarr, CE, 28 (1966), 67; Judd Arnold, SCN, 24
(1966), 10; C. G. Thayer, MP, 64 (1966), 74-6;
John J. Enck, MLR, 61 (1966), 673-4; Georges Bas,
Les Langues Moderne, 60 e année (1966), 468-9.

B94   Kronenberger, Louis. The Thread of Laughter: Chap-
      ters on English Stage Comedy from Jonson to
      Maugham. New York: Alfred A. Knopf, 1952.
      Reviewed: Francis Fergusson, Yale Rev., 42
      (1952), 289-90.

B95   Langsam, G. Geoffrey. Martial Books and Tudor
      Verse. New York: King's Crown Press (Columbia
      Univ.), 1951.
      Includes brief discussions of Every Man In,
      Every Man Out, and Poetaster.

B96   Leavis, F. R. "The Line of Wit," in Seventeenth-
      Century English Poetry, ed. W. R. Keast. New
      York: Oxford Univ. Press, 1962.

B97   LeComte, Edward. The Notorious Lady Essex. New
      York: Dial Press, 1969.
      Among others Jonson and Donne's associations
      with the Lady are discussed.

B98   Leech, Clifford. Shakespeare's Tragedies and Other
      Studies in Seventeenth Century Drama. London:
      Chatto and Windus, 1950.
      Republished in 1961, the book, of course, is not
      primarily concerned with Jonson, but his works are
      mentioned passim.

B99   Leishman, J. B. The Monarch of Wit. London:
      Hutchinson, 1951.
      Donne and Jonson wrote consciously for the in-
      tellectual minority.

B100 _____. The Art of Marvell's Poetry. London:
      Hutchinson, 1966.
      Assessment of Marvell's debt to Donne, Crashaw,

Crowley, Jonson, Spenser, Cleveland, and the
Ancients.

B101   Levin, Harry. The Myth of The Golden Age in the
Renaissance. Bloomington: Univ. of Indiana
Press, 1970.
Chapter V deals in part with Jonson.

B102   Literary English Since Shakespeare, ed. George Watson. Oxford: Oxford Univ. Press, 1970.
Contains an essay on Jonson's prose style.

B103   MacCarthy, Desmond, ed. Humanities. New York:
Oxford Univ. Press, 1954.
Brings together reviews, essays and articles,
covering the last quarter century. The essay included on Jonson is a review (first published in 1921)
of the Phoenix Society performance of Volpone.

B104   McCollom, William G. The Divine Average: A
View of Comedy. Cleveland: Case Western Re-
serve Univ. Press, 1971.
Contains a chapter entitled "On the Edge of
Comedy: Jonson's Bartholomew Fair. "

B105   Maclean, Hugh. "Ben Jonson's Poems: Notes on the
Ordered Society, " in Essays in English Literature
from the Renaissance to the Victorian Age. Presented to A. S. P. Woodhouse, ed. Millar Mac-
Lure and F. W. Watt. Toronto: Univ. of Toronto Press, 1964, pp. 43-68.
"I suggest that, while the plays deal principally
in the satiric recognition and description of the
factors that contribute to social disorder, we find
in the poems (with the Discoveries behind, as
theory to practice), not an explicit and detailed
outline of the social order Jonson admired, but
rather 'notes' on particular elements that ought to
mark a society properly ordered, as well as suggestions for conduct in the midst of a disordered
one" (pp. 44-45).

B106   Maddison, Carol. Apollo and the Nine: A History of
the Ode. London: Routledge and Kegan Paul, 1960.
The last part of the book is devoted to the
English Ode, including detailed examinations of
poems by Jonson and others.

B107 Mason, H. A. Humanism and Poetry in the Early
Tudor Period. London: Routledge and Kegan Paul,
1959.
Concentrates on the works of More, Wyatt, and
Jonson.

B108 Matchett, William H. The Phoenix and the Turtle:
Shakespeare's Poem and Chester's 'Loves Martyr'.
The Hague: Mouton, 1965.
Analyzes the poem in isolation, against Chester's poem, and with the poems by Jonson, Chapman, and Marston which accompanied Shakespeare's
poem in Robert Chester's volume.

B109 Meagher, John C. Method and Meaning in Jonson's
Masques. Notre Dame, Indiana: Univ. of Notre
Dame Press, 1966.
Reviewed: F. J. Hunter, QJS, 53 (1967), 84.

B110 Messiaen, Pierre. Theatre Anglais, Moyen-Age et
XVIe siècle: Anonymes, Marlowe, Dekker, Heywood, Ben Jonson, Webster, Tourneur.... Nou-
velle traduction française avec remarques et notes.
Paris: Desclée de Brouwer, 1948.

B111 Miles, Josephine. Eras and Modes in English Poetry. Berkeley: California Univ. Press, 1957;
Cambridge: Cambridge Univ. Press, 1957.
"The 17th century began with the clausal verse
of Jonson, Donne, and Herbert."

B112 Miner, Earl. The Cavalier Mode from Jonson to
Cotton. Princeton, N.J.: Princeton Univ. Press,
1971.
Reviewed: SCN, 30 (Summer, 1972), 36-38.

B113 Moore, Rayburn S. "Some Notes on the 'Courtly
Love' System in Jonson's The New Inn," in Essays
in Honor of W. C. Curry. Nashville: Vanderbilt
Univ. Press, 1954, pp. 133-42.

B114 Muir, Kenneth. Introduction to Elizabethan Litera-
ture. New York: Random House, 1967.
One chapter devoted to Lyly, Peele, Marlowe,
Greene, Lodge, Nashe, Kyd, and Jonson.

B115 Musgrove, Sydney. Shakespeare and Jonson. The

MacMillan Brown Lectures. New Zealand: Aukland Univ. College Bull. No. 51, English Series No. 9, Aukland, 1957.
Reviewed: G. E. Bentley, SQ, 9 (1958), 575; TLS, Feb. 14, 1958, p. 91 [brief].

B116   Nichols, J. G. The Poetry of Ben Jonson. New York: Barnes and Noble, Inc., 1969.

B117   Nicoll, Allardyce. "The Growth of Realistic Comedy: Ben Jonson," in World Drama from Aeschylus to Anouilh. New York: Harcourt-Brace, 1949, pp. 288-93.

B117a   _____. English Drama: A Modern Viewpoint. New York: Barnes and Noble, 1968.
Jonson is discussed in Chapter 5: "Jacobean Realism and Artificiality."

B118   Noyes, Robert Gale. Ben Jonson on the English Stage, 1660-1776. Philadelphia: Benjamin Blom, 1967.
Reprinted from 1935 edition (Harvard Studies in English, XVII).

B119   Olive, W. J. "Sejanus and Hamlet," in A Tribute to G. C. Taylor, ed. Arnold Williams. Chapel Hill: Univ. of North Carolina Press, 1952, pp. 178-84.

B120   Oras, Ants. Pause Patterns in Elizabethan and Jacobean Drama: An Experiment in Prosody. Univ. of Florida Monographs, Humanities, No. 3. Gainesville: Florida Univ. Press, 1960.
Contains short chapters on verse from Chaucer to Shakespeare, Jonson, and Donne.

B121   Orgel, Stephen. The Jonsonian Masque. Cambridge, Mass.: Harvard Univ. Press, 1965.
Reviewed: TLS, Aug. 26, 1965, p. 736; Ian Donaldson, RES, 17 (1966), 316-17; J. Leeds Barroll, RN, 19 (1966), 59-60.

B122   Ornstein, Robert. The Moral Vision of Jacobean Tragedy. Madison: Wisconsin Univ. Press, 1960.
Includes detailed studies of Chapman, Jonson, Tourneur, and Shakespeare.

B123   Palmer, Ralph Graham. Seneca's 'De Remediis
        Fortuitorum' and the Elizabethans. Chicago: In-
        stitute of Elizabethan Studies, 1953.
        Jonson and Marston adapt passages from De
        Remediis to their purposes.

B124   Parr, Johnstone. Tamburlaine's Malady and Other
        Essays on Astrology in Elizabethan Drama. Univ.,
        Ala.: Univ. of Alabama Press, 1953.
        Contains "Non-Alchemical Pseudo-Sciences in
        The Alchemist, " pp. 107-11 (first published in PQ,
        24 (1945), 85-89); and Bibliographical Survey,
        p. 112-150.

B125   Partridge, A. C. The Accidence of Ben Jonson's
        Plays, Masques, and Entertainments. With an
        Appendix of Comparable Uses in Shakespeare.
        Cambridge: Bowes and Bowes, 1953.
        An historical account of the morphology of Jon-
        son's plays, masques, and entertainments.
        Reviewed: E. G. Stanley, MLR, 49 (1954),
        368-9; Mark Eccles, JEGP, 54 (1955), 283 [brief];
        Hereward T. Price, SQ, 6 (1955), 102-3; Hermann
        Heuer, SJ, 90 (1954), 345-7; E. J. Dobson, RES,
        6 (1955), 197-201.

B125a   _____ . Studies in the Syntax of Ben Jonson's
        Plays. Cambridge: Bowes and Bowes, 1953.
        See B125 for reviews.

B126   _____ . Orthography in Shakespeare and Elizabethan
        Drama: A Study of Colloquial Contractions, Eli-
        sion, Prosody and Punctuation. London: Arnold,
        1964.
        Jonson favored a logical system of punctuation;
        Shakespeare, a rhythmical one.

B127   Partridge, Edward B. The Broken Compass: A
        Study of the Major Comedies of Ben Jonson. Lon-
        don: Chatto and Windus, 1958; Cambridge, Mass.:
        Harvard Univ. Press, 1958.
        "This study of Jonson's imagery tries to re-
        veal how his imagination works in his major
        comedies" (p. 18).
        Reviewed: John Daniel, Manchester Guar.
        Weekly, Oct. 23, 1958, p. 10; New Statesman,
        Nov. 29, 1958, pp. 772-3; Kenneth Muir, London

114   Ben Jonson Bibliography

Mag., 5, No. 2 (1959), 77-8; W. W. Robson,
Spectator, Jan. 9, 1959, p. 51; J. J. Enck, RN,
12 (1959), 119-21; H. Feinstein, QJS, 45 (1959),
336-7; C. G. Thayer, BA, 33 (1959), 219; M.
Poirier, Etudes Anglaises, 12 (1959), 350; G. K.
Hunter, EIC, 9 (1959), 406-11; M. T. Herrick,
JEGP, 58 (1959), 528-30; Quar. Rev. No. 619
(Jan. 1959), 119-20; J. A. Bryant, Jr., Sewanee
Rev., 67 (1959), 700; TLS, Feb. 20, 1959, p. 98;
Aerol Arnold, Personalist, 41 (1960), 245; R. L.
Clubb, CL, 11 (1960), 89-90; John S. Baxter, QQ,
67 (1960), 313-4.

B128   Pennanen, Esko V. Chapters on the Language of Ben
Jonson's Dramatic Works. Annales Universitatis
Turkuensis, Series B., 39. Turku, 1951.
     Pennanen concludes (p. 203): "In other words,
Jonson speaks to us most immediately through his
style; the words do not matter so much as the
ends he made them serve. And that is how an
extensive study of Jonson's language enables us to
enjoy his art more fully by developing in us an
ability to see behind the scenes of his mind."
     Reviewed: E. G. Stanley, MLR, 49 (1954),
368-9.

B129   _____. Notes on the Grammar in Ben Jonson's
Dramatic Works. Acta Academiae Socialis, Ser.
A., Vol. 3 (1966).

B130   Phelps, Gilbert. "Ben Jonson's Poetry," in Guide to
Eng. Lit. Vol. III, ed. Boris Ford. Baltimore:
Penguin Books, 1956, 131-41.

B131   Praz, Mario. "Ben Jonson's Italy," The Flaming
Heart: Essays on Crashaw, Machiavelli, and
Other Studies in the Relations Between Italian and
English Literature from Chaucer to T. S. Eliot.
New York: Doubleday and Co., Inc., 1958,
pp. 168-85.

B132   Puttenham, George. The Arte of English Poesie.
Menston: Scolar Press, 1968.
     Unique for being reproduced from Ben Jonson's
copy.

B133   [Quinn, Edward.]   "Jonson, Ben[jamin] (1572-1637), "
       in The Reader's Encyclopedia of World Drama, ed.
       John Gassner. New York: Thomas Y. Crowell
       Company, 1969. pp. 494-96.
       In addition to this biographical entry, there are
       brief entries for some of the major plays (The Al-
       chemist, pp. 12-13; Bartholomew Fair, p. 52;
       Epicoene, p. 250; Volpone, p. 901); and elsewhere
       Jonson is mentioned in passing, as in the entry
       for "Pastoral Drama" (p. 642).

B134   Rajan, B. and A. G. George, eds. Makers of Liter-
       ary Criticism, Vol. 1. Asia Publishing House,
       1966.
       English critics include Jonson.

B135   Redwine, James D. Jr., ed. Ben Jonson's Literary
       Criticism. Regents Critics Series. Lincoln:
       Univ. of Nebraska Press, 1970.

B136   Reed, Robert Rentoul, Jr. The Occult on the Tudor
       and Stuart Stage. Boston: The Christopher Pub-
       lishing House, 1965.
       Contains discussions of Epicoene, Oberon, The
       Faery Prince, The Alchemist, The Masques of
       Queenes, The Sad Shepherd, The Entertainment at
       Althrope, and The Devil Is An Ass.

B137   [Ribner, Irving.]   "Jonson, Ben[jamin] (1572-1637), "
       in The Reader's Encyclopedia of Shakespeare, ed.
       Oscar James Campbell and Edward G. Quinn.
       New York: Thomas Y. Crowell Company, 1966,
       pp. 406-08.

B138   Rich, Barnaby. Faultes, Faults, and Nothing Else
       But Faultes, ed. Melvin H. Wolf. Gainsville,
       Florida: Scholars' Facsimiles and Reprints, 1965.
       Notes correspondences of Rich's satire with
       Jonson's.

B139   Roberts, S. C., ed. Essays and Reflections by
       Harold Child. Cambridge: Cambridge Univ.
       Press, 1948.
       Includes "The Triumph of Ben Jonson. "

B140   Robinson, Edwin Arlington. Ben Jonson Entertains
       a Man from Stratford, trans. by Stanistaw

Helsztyński into Polish. Warszawa: Towarzystwo
Przyjaciót Książki (Ass'n. of Bibliophiles), 1968.

B141   Ryan, A. P., ed. Critics Who have Influenced Taste.
Bles., reprinted from The [London] Times, 1965.
"Survey of writers, from Jonson onwards,
whose critical criteria and judgments have exer-
cised a decisive influence on the opinions and
tastes of the reading public of their time."

B142   Sackton, Alexander H. Rhetoric As A Dramatic Language in Ben Jonson. New York: Columbia Univ.
Press, 1948.
Reprinted in 1967, "this study attempts to
describe in detail certain values which Jonson
created with rhetoric. In his plays rhetoric becomes a dramatic language through which he com-
municates indirectly with his audience. I have
chosen jargon and the language of hyperbole for
special analysis because they are prominent and
recognized characteristics of Jonson's style, and
representative forms of language to which Jonson
gave a distinct rhetorical aim" (p. vii).
Reviewed: Marcia L. Anderson, SAQ, 48
(1949), 156; Sr. Miriam Joseph, JEGP, 48 (1949),
409-11; D. C. Bryant, QJS, 35 (1949), 94-5; R.
G. Cox, Scrutiny, 16 (1949), 71-4; C. T. Harrison, Sewanee Rev., 57 (1949), 709-14; J. Gerritsen, ES, 31 (1950), 223-4; A. K. McIlwraith,
RES, N. Ser. I (1950), 167-8; E. W. Talbert,
MLQ, 12 (1951), 110-11.

B143   Salmon, Vivian. "Language-Planning in Seventeenth-
Century England: Its Context and Aims," in In
Memory of J. R. Firth, ed. C. E. Bazell, J. C.
Catford, M. A. K. Halliday, and R. H. Robins.
New York: Longmans, 1966.
Supplies biographical notes on Henry Reynolds,
who overspent on staging Jonson's Masque of
Queens for James I.

B144   Sansom, Clive. The World of Poetry: Poets and
Critics on the Art and Functions of Poetry.
Phoenix House, 1959.
Jonson is one of the many poets included in the
selected extracts.

B145   Sanvic, Romain. Le Théâtre élisabéthain. Brussells:
        Office de Publicité, S. A., Editeurs, 1955.
        Discusses Shakespeare's predecessors and suc-
        cessors, including Jonson.

B146   Savage, James E. The 'Conceited Newes' of Sir
        Thomas Overbury and His Friends. A Facsimile
        Reproduction with a Commentary and Textual Notes
        on the 'Newes.' Gainesville, Florida: Scholars'
        Facsimiles and Reprints, 1968.
        Recreates many of the circumstances of the
        composition of the 'Newes' from a poem of Jon-
        son's.

B147   Schelling, Felix. "Ben Jonson and the Classical
        School, " in Essential Articles for the Study of
        English Augustan Backgrounds, ed. Bernard N.
        Schilling. Hamden, Conn.: The Shoe String Press,
        1961.
        Schelling's article was originally published in
        PMLA, 1898.

B148   Schlüter, Kurt von. Die englische Ode: Studien zu
        ihrer Entwicklung unter dem Einfluss der antiken
        Hymne. Bonn: H. Bouvier und Co., 1964.
        Analyzes odes from Jonson to the Romantics.

B149   Schoenbaum, Samuel. "Shakespeare and Jonson:
        Fact and Myth, " in The Elizabethan Theatre, II,
        ed. David Galloway. Hamden, Conn.: Archon
        Books, 1970, pp. 1-19.

B150   _____ . Shakespeare's Lives. Oxford: The
        Clarendon Press, 1970.
        See especially the section entitled "Shakespeare
        vs. Jonson, " pp. 92-7.

B151   Schücking, Levin L. von. Shakespeare und der
        Tragödienstil seiner Zeit. Bern: A. Francke Ag.
        Verlag., 1948.
        Examination of Shakespeare's work against the
        background of the efforts of his contemporaries;
        includes interpretations of tragic heroes in Mar-
        lowe, Chapman, Webster, and Jonson.

B152   Sellin, Paul R. Daniel Heinsius and Stuart England.
        Leiden: At the Univ. Press, 1968; London: Ox-

ford Univ. Press, 1968.
Contains discussion of Jonson's response to
Heinsius' treatise on tragedy and other matters of
literary criticism.
Reviewed: George C. Schoolfield, SCN, 30
(1972), 14-15.

B153   Seymour-Smith, Martin. Poets Through Their Letters.
Vol. I: Wyatt to Coleridge. London: Constable,
1969.
Includes discussion of Jonson among those poets
who have not left any large number of revealing
letters behind them.

B154   Simmonds, James D. Masques of God: Form and
Theme in the Poetry of Henry Vaughan. Pitts-
burgh: Univ. of Pittsburgh Press, 1972.
Chapter II of this study is entitled "Ben Jonson
and the Craft of Poetry."
Reviewed: Martin E. Itzkowitz, SCN, 30 (Fall-
Winter, 1972), 57-8.

B155   Simonini, R. C., Jr. Italian Scholarship in Renaissance England. Chapel Hill: Univ. of North Carolina Press, 1952.
Last chapter discusses the debt of Shakespeare
and Jonson to contemporary teachers of Italian.

B156   Simpson, Percy. "The Art of Ben Jonson," in Essays and Studies by Members of the English Asso-
ciation, Vol. 30 (1944). Collected by C. H. Wil-
kinson. Oxford: Clarendon Press, 1945, pp. 35-
49.

B157   _____. Studies in Elizabethan Drama. Oxford:
The Clarendon Press, 1955.
Includes an essay on Jonson's art.

B158   Sisson, C. J. "A Topical Reference in The Alchemist," in John Quincy Adams: Memorial Studies.
Washington, D.C.: Folger Shakespeare Lib.,
1948, pp. 739-41.
Evidence given in Chancery in Nov.-Feb. 1609-
10 tells the story of Sir Anthony and Saul Asheley,
who used one Greene to bilk the "very phantasticall
and humorous" Thomas Rogers by promising an introduction and marriage to the Queen of the Fairies.

B159 Stagg, Louis C. Index to the Figurative Language of
      Ben Jonson's Tragedies. Charlottesville: Biblio.
      Soc. of the Univ. of Virginia, 1967.

B160 Starnes, DeWitt T. and Ernest William Talbert.
      Classical Myth and Legend in Renaissance Dic-
      tionaries: A Study of Renaissance Dictionaries in
      their Relation to the Classical Learning of Con-
      temporary English Writers. Chapel Hill: Univ.
      of North Carolina Press, 1955; Cambridge: Ox-
      ford Univ. Press, 1955.

B160a Sternfeld, Frederick W. "Song in Jonson's Comedy:
      A Gloss on Volpone." Studies in the Eng. Renais-
      sance Drama, ed. Josephine W. Bennett, Oscar
      Cargill, and Vernon Hall, Jr. New York: N.Y.
      Univ. Press, 1959, pp. 310-21.

B161 Stoll, Elmer Edgar. Poets and Playwrights: Shake-
      speare, Jonson, Spenser, Milton. Minneapolis:
      Univ. of Minn. Press, 1967 reprint; originally
      published 1930.
      Reviewed: SCN, 26 (1968), 43.

B162 Swinburne, Algernon Charles. A Study of Ben Jon-
      son, ed. and introd. by Howard B. Norland.
      Lincoln: Univ. of Nebraska Press, 1969.
      New edition of Swinburne's original work.

B163 Syme, Ronald. "Roman Historians and Renaissance
      Politics," in Society and History in the Renaissance.
      A report of a conference held at the Folger Li-
      brary on April 23 and 24, 1960, pp. 3-12.
      Through Jonson he links Tacitus and Machia-
      velli.

B164 Tannenbaum, Samuel A. and Dorothy R. Tannenbaum.
      Supplement to A Concise Bibliography of Ben Jon-
      son. New York: 1947.

B165 Taylor, Dick, Jr. "Clarendon and Ben Jonson as
      Witnesses for the Earl of Pembroke's Character,"
      in Studies in the English Renaissance Drama, ed.
      Josephine W. Bennett, Oscar Cargill, and Vernon
      Hall, Jr. New York: New York University Press,
      1959, pp. 322-44.

B166   Taylor, George C. "Did Shakespeare, Actor, Impro-
       vise in Every Man In His Humour?" in John
       Quincy Adams Memorial Studies, ed. J. G.
       McManaway, G. E. Dawson, and E. A. Willoughby.
       Washington, D.C.: The Folger Shakespeare Li-
       brary, 1948.

B167   Thayer, C. G. Ben Jonson: Studies in the Plays.
       Norman: Univ. of Oklahoma Press, 1963.
       "In the present book I have dealt primarily with
       Jonson's arguments, secondarily with his art; to
       deal with both adequately would require more than
       one large volume. Strongly ethical in bent, very
       much the moralist, Jonson, like other moralists,
       chose satirical comedy as his primary mode of
       dramatic discourse. What the discourse is about
       is the subject of the following pages" (p. vii).
       Reviewed: Waldo F. MacNeir, CL, 15 (1963),
       183-6; T. A. Stroud, Sat. Rev., June 15, 1963,
       p. 43; TLS, (1963), p. 594; J. J. Enck, RN, 16
       (1963), 345f.; Waldo F. McNeir, BA, 38.1 (1964),
       74; Eugene M. Waith, SEL, 4.2 (1964), 327-8.

B168   Tiedje, Egon. Die Tradition Ben Jonsons in der
       Restaurationskomödie, Hamburg: Cram, de Gruy-
       fer & Co., 1963.
       Reviewed: Dieter Mehl, Archiv f Stud., 203
       (1966), 145-7; Lothar Hönnighausen, Anglia, 82
       (1964), 124-25; Gunnar Sorelius, Studia Neophilo-
       logica, 36 (1964), 355-57.

B169   Townsend, Freda L. Apologie for Bartholomew
       Fayre: The Art of Jonson's Comedies. New
       York: The Modern Language Assoc. of Amer.,
       1947.
       "This study opposes itself to the classical por-
       trait of an Elizabethan playwright. Jonson, pro-
       ponent of art and labor, is reconciled with Jonson,
       prodigal playwright, by taking new measure of his
       art" (Preface, p. vi).
       Reviewed: Percy Simpson, RES, 24 (1948),
       253-4; M. T. Herrick, JEGP, 47 (1948), 305-6;
       D. J. Gordon, MLR, 44 (1949), 110; D. C.
       Boughner, MLN, 44 (1949), 135-7; J. Gerritsen,
       ES, 31 (1950), 183-4; A. K. McIlwraith, RES, N.
       Ser. I (1950), 166-7.

B170   Trimpi, Wesley.   Ben Jonson's Poems: A Study of
        the Plain Style.   Palo Alto: Stanford Univ. Press,
        1962.
           Reviewed: V. de S.   Pinto, Critical Quar. , 5
        (1963), 180-1; Arnold Stein, ELH, 30 (1963), 306-
        16; Ralph Lawrence, English, 14 (1963), 246; TLS,
        1963, p. 594; Hugh Maclean, UTQ, 33 (1963), 89-
        97; Lester A. Beaurline, Virginia Quar. Rev. , 39
        (1963), 341-4; John Buxton, Archiv. f. Stud. ,
        201.3 (1964), 216-8; J. J. Enck, MLR, 59.1
        (1964), 106; J. A. Barish, MP, 61.3 (1964), 240-
        3; Sanford Golding, JEGP, 63.1 (1964), 166-8; E.
        B. Partridge, RN, 17.4 (1964), 348-50; George W.
        Williams, SAQ, 63.1 (1964), 116-7; but see es-
        pecially Arnold Stein, ELH, 30 (1963), 306-16
        (Item No. A418 above).

B171   Ure, Peter.   "Shakespeare and the Drama of his
        Time: IV Jonson and The Satirists, " in A New
        Companion to Shakespeare Studies, ed. Kenneth
        Muir and S. Schoenbaum.   Cambridge: Cambridge
        University Press, 1971, pp. 216-18.

B172   Wada, Yuichi.   Ben Jonson.   Tokyo: Kenkyusha,
        1963.

B173   Wallis, Lawrence B.   Fletcher, Beaumont and Com-
        pany: Entertainers to the Jacobean Gentry.   New
        York: King's Crown Press, 1947; London: Ox-
        ford Univ. Press, 1947.
           Shakespeare and Jonson receive tangential treat-
        ment, as the "and company."

B174   Walton, Geoffrey, "The Tone of Ben Jonson's Poetry,"
        in Seventeenth-Century English Poetry: Modern
        Essays in Criticism, ed. William R. Keast.   New
        York: Oxford Univ. Press, 1962, pp. 193-214.
           Attempts "to locate and define as clearly as
        possible" Jonson's "characteristic tone and civi-
        lized quality" (p. 194).

B175   _____.   Metaphysical to Augustan.   London:
        Bowes and Bowes, 1955.
           Contains a chapter on the tone of Ben Jonson's
        poetry, showing that he anticipated the Augustans;
        see B174.

B176   Weimann, Robert, ed.   Dramen der Shakespearezeit.
        Leipzig: Dieterich'schen Verlagsbuchhandlung,
        1964.
            Includes Jonson's Volpone translated into Ger-
        man.

B177   Wells, Stanley.   Literature and Drama With Special
        Reference to Shakespeare and His Contemporaries.
        London: Routledge and Kegan Paul, 1970.
            Includes discussion of Jonson.

B178   White, Harold Ogden.   Plagiarism and Imitation dur-
        ing the English Renaissance: A Study in Critical
        Distinctions.   New York: Octagon Books, 1965.
            From Cox to Jonson's Timber.   Originally pub-
        lished by Harvard Univ. Press in 1935.

B179   [no entry]

B180   Williamson, George.   "The Rhetorical Pattern of Neo-
        Classical Wit, " in Seventeenth Century Contexts,
        ed. George Williamson.   London: Faber & Faber,
        1960 (revised 1969), pp. 240-71.

B181   Wimsatt, William K.   See Brooks, Cleanth (B22).

B182   Winters, Ivor.   Forms of Discovery: Critical and
        Historical Essays on the Short Poem in English.
        Chicago: A. Swallow, 1967.
            Discussions of Jonson's poetry throughout.

B183   Wright, Louis B. and Virginia A. LaMar.   The
        Play's the Thing: Seventeen of Shakespeare's
        Greatest Dramas.   New York: Harper and Row,
        1963.
            Contains an appendix of early Shakespeare
        criticism from Ben Jonson to Sam Johnson.

DISSERTATIONS AND THESES

D1 Allen, Richard Ottaway. "Jacobean Drama and the
    Literature of Decay: A Study of Conservative Reac-
    tion in Literature" (Univ. of Michigan). DA, 30
    (1970), 3899-3900-A.
    A critical study of Jacobean coterie drama "(the
    drama produced by Webster, Tourneur, Chapman,
    Jonson, Marston and Middleton during the period
    1596 to 1616): its apocalyptic scene, its dissoci-
    ated, self-dramatizing hero, and its tragic and
    comic distinctions."

D2 Anderson, Mark Andrew. "Jonson's Criticism of So-
    ciety: Development in the Major Comedies" (Univ.
    of Wisconsin). DA, 29 (1969), 4448-A.

D3 Arnold, Hans Stephan. "The Reception of Ben Jonson,
    Beaumont and Fletcher, and Massinger in Eighteenth
    Century Germany" (Univ. of Maryland). DA, 26
    (1966), 3323-4.

D4 Arnold, Judd Baldwin. "Form and Meaning in the
    Comedies of Ben Jonson" (Univ. of Connecticut).
    DA, 26 (1966), 5408.

D5 Balestri, Charles Angelo. "English Neoclassicism and
    Shakespeare: A Study in Conflicting Ideas of Drama-
    tic Form" (Yale Univ., 1970). DAI, 31 (1971),
    6537-A.
    This study contrasts "Jonson's and Shakespeare's
    response to the classical model" discussing "its
    place in their respective dramaturgies."

D6 Barker, Walter L. "Three English Pantalones: A
    Study in Relations Between the Commedia Dell'arte
    and Elizabethan Drama" (Univ. of Connecticut). DA,
    27 (1967), 3419-A.

123

D7   Bauer, Robert V. "The Use of Humors in Comedy by
     Ben Jonson and his Contemporaries" (Univ. of Illi-
     nois, 1948).

D8   Benn, C. DeC. W. "Ben Jonson and Inigo Jones: The
     Problem of Artistic Collaboration in Stuart Masques"
     (MA Thesis, University College, English, Univ. of
     London, 1951).

D9   Bocan, Sister Agnes, SS.C.M. "Nature and Art
     Themes in the Middle Comedies of Ben Jonson"
     (Univ. of Notre Dame, 1970). DAI, 31 (1971), 4705-
     A.

D10 Brock, Dewey Heyward. "Poet and Society: A Criti-
     cal Study of Ben Jonson's Concept of Society in the
     Light of Classical and Christian Ideals" (Univ. of
     Kansas, 1969). DAI, 30 (1970), 5440-A.

D11 Burns, Robert Lee. "A Critical Study of Thomas
     Middleton's Early Realistic Comedies" (Univ. of
     Louisville, 1969). DAI, 31 (1970), 2335-A.
        Measures Middleton's accomplishments against
     those of Jonson and Shakespeare.

D12 Cain, Thomas Henry. "The Poem of Compliment in
     the English Renaissance" (Univ. of Wisconsin, 1959).
     DA, 20 (1959), 2285.
        See pp. 249-264: "Ben Jonson: A Major Poet
     of Compliment, " and also pp. 296-303, which deal
     with "Jonson's To Penshurst. "

D13 Campbell, Marian Selma Johnson. "The Beginnings of
     the English Comedy of Manners in the Renaissance"
     (Univ. of Colorado, 1971). DAI, 32 (1972), 3944-A.

D14 Chalfant, Fran Cernocky. "Ben Jonson's London: The
     Plays, The Masques, and The Poems" (Univ. of
     North Carolina, Chapel Hill, 1971). DAI, 32 (1972),
     6922-A.
        "The intent of this study is to show that Jonson
     put his knowledge of the city which was virtually
     his lifetime home to the same didactic and enter-
     taining purposes as his command of classical and
     medieval matter. This is achieved by collecting
     and commenting upon all of the London place-names
     mentioned in his plays, masques, and poems. "

D15   Champion, Larry Stephen.   "The Comic Intent of Ben
        Jonson's Late Plays" (Univ. of North Carolina,
        1961). DA, 22 (1962), 2784-5.

D16   Chapman, Mildred Shows.   "Ben Jonson and the Court"
        (Louisiana State Univ.). DA, 30 (1970), 2961-62-A.

D17   Christopher, Georgia B.   "A Study of the Jonsonian,
        Pastoral, and Apocalyptic Strains in Silex Scintillans"
        (Yale Univ.). DA, 27 (1967), 4217-8-A.

D18   Clearman, Mary Rebecca Hogeland.   "Aspects of Juve-
        nal in Ben Jonson's Comical Satires (Univ. of Mis-
        souri). DA, 30 (1970), 4939-A.

D19   Clubb, Roger Lane.   "The Relationship of Language to
        Character in Ben Jonson's Every Man Out of His
        Humour (Yale Univ. 1958-59). DA, 30 (1969), 274-A.

D20   Cohen, Gerald.   "A Comparative Evaluation of the
        Pastoral Tradition in English and French Literature
        in the Early Seventeenth Century" (Univ. of Washing-
        ton). DA, 20 (1959), 1011-2.
          William Browne, John Fletcher, Ben Jonson,
        John Milton, etc.

D21   Cone, Mary.   "Fletcher Without Beaumont: A Study of
        the Independent Plays of John Fletcher" (Univ. of
        Mississippi, 1970). DAI, 31 (1971), 4760-A.
          Fletcher followed the example set by Jonson's
        early comedies: "Jonson in his 'comicall satyre'
        and Fletcher in almost all of his plays clarified the
        roles of satirists with statements of purpose by the
        characters themselves. "

D22   Connor, Rodney Vincent.   "A Study of Ben Jonson's
        Comedies: The Comic Perspectives" (Univ. of
        Washington, 1962). DA, 23 (1963), 4341-2.

D23   Cook, E.   "The Tribe of Ben. " M. Litt. Thesis, Cam-
        bridge, England, 1950.

D24   Cornelia, Sister M. Bonaventure, SS. J.   "The Func-
        tion of the Masque in Jacobean Tragedy and Tragi-
        comedy" (Fordham Univ.). DA, 29 (1969), 2705-A.

D25   Couillard, Theophane Venard.   "Anti-Puritan Satire in

Ben Jonson's Dramatic Works" (Univ. of Colorado,
1967). DA, 28 (1968), 3634-A.
"From first to last Jonson levels scathing invec-
tive against what he supposes the anti-intellectual
and materialistic Puritan values in such sharp contrast with his own. "

D26   Crupi, Charles William.   "Pastoral Elements in Plays
from the Elizabethan Public Theaters of the 1950's"
(Princeton Univ., 1967).   DA, 28 (1968), 3175-76-A.

D27   Cubeta, Paul M.   "A Critical Study of Ben Jonson's
Non-Dramatic Poetry" (Yale Univ., 1954).

D28   Curry, Rev. John Vincent, S.J.   "Deception in Elizabethan Comedy: An Analytical Study" (Columbia
Univ., 1951).

D29   Dale, Leona Ford.   "Health Imagery and Rhetoric in
the Major Comedies of Ben Jonson (Texas Techni-
cal Univ.).   DA, 30 (1970), 3427-A.

D30   De Luna, Barbara Nielson.   "Jonson's Romish Plot:
A Study of Catiline and Its Historical Content"
(State Univ. Iowa, 1963).   DA, 24 (1963), 740.
Note: This dissertation was published in 1967 by
the Oxford Press.

D31   Demaray, John G.   "Comus as a Masque" (Columbia
Univ.).   DA, 28 (1967), 624-A.

D32   Denniston, Elliott Averett.   "Jonson's Bartholomew
Fair and the Jacobean Stage" (Univ. of Michigan,
1970).   DAI, 32 (1971), 424-A.

D33   De Sante, Rev. Paul John.   "An Analysis of the Antimasque in the Court Masques of Ben Jonson" (St.
John's, 1962-63).

D34   Dessen, Alan Charles.   "Ben Jonson and the Estates
Morality Tradition" (Johns Hopkins, 1962-63).

D35   Dowling, Linda Crabill.   "Ben Jonson, his Learned
Hand and True Promethean Art: A Study of the
Non-Dramatic Poetry" (Brown Univ., 1970).   DAI,
32 (1971), 3247-A.
Places particular emphasis upon "the fundamental-

ly social nature of Jonson's concerns in the non-
dramatic poems. "

D36   Drew-Bear, Annette.   "Rhetoric in Ben Jonson's Middle
      Plays: A Study of Ethos, Character Portrayal, and
      Persuasion" (Univ. of Wisconsin, 1971). DAI, 32
      (1971), 2054-A.
      Examines Jonson's rhetorical method in four
      plays: Sejanus, Volpone, Alchemist, and Bart. Fair.

D37   Dudley, Leonea Barbour.   "The Language of Comedy:
      An Introductory Analysis of the Verbal Forms of the
      Comic Spirit in Drama" (Cornell Univ.). Abstracts
      of Theses, 1944, 37-42.
      Examines The Alchemist as the representative
      comedy of the Jacobean period.

D38   Earley, Robert Schafer.   "Ben Jonson's Epigrammes:
      A Study in Convention" (Rutgers Univ., 1972). DAI,
      33 (1972), 1721-A.

D39   Enck, John J.   "Ben Jonson's Imagery" (Diss., Har-
      vard Univ., 1951).

D40   English, Hubert M., Jr.   "Prosody and Meaning in
      Ben Jonson's Poems" (Diss., Yale Univ., 1955).

D41   Evans, K. W.   "Ben Jonson and the Idea of a Common-
      wealth" (M. A. Thesis, Univ. of Wales, Swansea,
      1966-67).

D42   Field, Michael Jay.   "Alternate Design: A Study of
      the Interaction of Theme and Structure in Ben Jon-
      son's Poetry" (Cornell Univ.). DA, 31 (1970),
      1273-A.
      By discussion of "On the Famous Voyage" and
      "To the Immortal Memorie, and Friendship of that
      Noble Paire, Sir Lucius Cary, and Sir H. Morison"
      demonstrates that Jonson considered the structural
      problems of poetry as essentially moral problems
      and the writing of poetry a moral act.

D43   Flower, Annette Chappell.   "The Disguised Prince in
      English Drama, 1590-1615" (Univ. of Maryland,
      1970). DAI, 31 (1971), 6054-A.
      Bartholomew Fair is used by way of example.

D44   Fredeman, Patsy Dale Hines. "Ben Jonson: Princi-
       ples of Criticism and Creation" (Univ. of Oklahoma,
       1972). DAI, 33 (1972), 1140-A.
       Attempts to deal satisfactorily with Jonson's
       "mastery of forms, the principles of which have
       been misunderstood, as has his point of view which
       is hidden behind the indirectness of satire. "

D45   Freeman, R. "The Theme of Parenthood in Some
       Elizabethan and Jacobean Plays, With Particular
       Reference to Kyd, Marston, Shakespeare, and Jon-
       son" (M. Phil. Thesis, University College, Univ.
       of London, 1967-68).

D46   Furniss, Warren Todd. "Ben Jonson's Masques and
       Entertainments" (Diss., Yale Univ., 1952).

D47   Gardiner, Judith Kegan. "Craftsmanship in Context:
       Ben Jonson's Poetry" (Columbia Univ.). DA, 30
       (1970), 3457-58-A.

D48   Gianakaris, Constantine John. "Humanistic Thought
       and the Moment of Judgment in Ben Jonson's
       Comedies" (Univ. of Wisconsin, 1961). DA, 22
       (1961), 1976-7.

D49   Gottwald, M. "Ben Jonson's Comic Theory and Prac-
       tice, with Specific Reference to his Satiric Purpose"
       (M. A. Thesis, Univ. of Birmingham, 1959).

D50   Graham, Hugh R. "Ben Jonson's Didactic Tragedies,
       Sejanus and Catiline" (Temple Univ.). DA, 27
       (1967), 3455-A.

D51   Grow, Gerald O. "Paradise Lost and The Renaissance
       Drama: Milton's Theme of Fall and its Dramatic
       Counterpart in Marlowe, Shakespeare, Jonson, and
       Middleton" (Yale Univ.). DA, 30 (1969), 723-24-A.

D52   Gum, Coburn. "The Aristophanic Comedies of Ben
       Jonson" (Duke Univ., 1962). DA, 23 (1963), 4679-
       80.

D53   Hahamovitch, Lillian. "An Approach to the Non-
       Dramatic Poetry of Ben Jonson" (Univ. of Miami,
       1970). DAI, 31 (1971), 4715-A.

D54   Hammood, Emily Evans. "A Directorial Analysis of
      Ben Jonson's Volpone" (Case Western Reserve Univ.,
      1972). DAI, 33 (1972), 1878-A.
      This theater thesis concludes "that Jonson's
      dramatic purpose can be fulfilled theatrically by the
      director who first recognizes that Volpone's incredi-
      bly complex design restricts creative experimenta-
      tion. "

D55   Hawkins, Harriet B. "Five Poetic Worlds: A Study
      of the Relationship between Thematic Content and
      Dramatic Construction in Representative Works of
      Ben Jonson" (Washington Univ.). DA, 26 (1965), 355.

D56   Haworth, W. "Ben Jonson's Criticism: A Study of
      its Place in the Development of English Literary
      Criticism in the Sixteenth and Seventeenth Centuries,
      Up to 1650" (M. A. Thesis, Univ. of Manchester,
      England, 1957).

D57   Henke, James Thomas. "Elizabethan-Jacobean Dramatic
      Bawdy: A Glossary and Critical Essay" (Univ. of
      Washington, 1970). DAI, 32 (1971), 389-A.

D58   Holt, Albert Hamilton. "The Nature of the Dramatic
      Illusion and its Violations in Jonson's Comedies--
      His Precedents in Theory and Practice" (Vanderbilt
      Univ.). DA, 18 (1958), 1786-87.

D59   Houck, Joseph Kemp. "Rhetorical Motifs in Ben Jon-
      son's Early Comedy, With Special Reference to
      Epicoene" (Univ. of North Carolina). DA, 28 (1968),
      3672-3-A.

D60   Houser, David John. "The Tradition of Honesty in
      Elizabethan and Jacobean Drama" (Univ. of Wiscon-
      sin). DAI, 31 (1970), 359-60-A.
      Bartholomew Fair is one of eight plays discussed.

D61   Humez, Jean McMahon. "The Manners of Epigram:
      A Study of the Epigram Volumes of Martial, Haring-
      ton, and Jonson" (Yale Univ., 1971). DAI, 32
      (1972), 6931-A.

D62   Hunt, Effie N. "Ben Jonson's Five-Act Structure"
      (Univ. of Illinois). Microfilm Abstracts, 10 (1950),
      26-7.

D63   Johnson, Nell E. "Jonson's Ovidian Elegies with Par-
      ticular Attention to the Underwood XXIX--'The Ex-
      postulation' Controversy" (Univ. of Colorado). DA,
      28 (1967), 1436-7-A.

D64   Johnston, Elizabeth Carrington. "The English Masque
      and the French Court Ballet, 1581-1640" (Harvard
      Univ., 1963-64).

D65   Jones, Robert Charles. "Well-made Men and Men-
      making Poets: Ben Jonson and the Problem of the
      Poet as a Teacher of Men" (Harvard Univ., 1963-64).

D66   Kay, W. David. "Ben Jonson, Horace, and the
      Poetomachia: The Development of an Elizabethan
      Playwright's Public Image" (Princeton Univ.). DA,
      29 (Jan.-Mar. 1969), 2713-A.

D67   Kennedy, Dennis Edward. "Character and Disguise in
      Ben Jonson's Major Plays" (Univ. of California,
      Santa Barbara, 1972). DAI, 33 (1972), 2381-A.

D68   Krishnappa, Josephine Balamani. "The Development of
      Jonson's Major Comedies" (Case Western Reserve).
      DA, 30 (1970), 3909-10-A.

D69   Lafkidon, Aliki. "The Aristophanic Spirit in the Come-
      dies of Ben Jonson" (Univ. of Denver, 1971). DAI,
      32 (1971), 2059-A.
         "The results of the study show that Jonson was not
      a close imitator of Aristophanes' art but that he was
      definitely influenced by his spirit, serious and merry."

D70   Langvardt, Arthur LeRoy. "The Verse Epigram in
      England during the Sixteenth and Early Seventeenth
      Centuries" (Univ. of Colorado, 1956). DA, 17
      (1957), 2595.

D71   Lawson, Anita Saffels. "In Dispraise of Folly: Sa-
      tiric Themes and Techniques in Selected Plays of
      Chapman, Jonson, and Marston, 1597-1606" (Tu-
      lane Univ., 1971). DAI, 32 (1971), 971-A.
         Takes into consideration Every Man In, Every
      Man Out, and Volpone.

D72   Levin, Lawrence Lee. "Justice and Justice Figures in
      Jonson" (Univ. of Wisconsin). DA, 30 (1969), 1141-A.

"Jonson demonstrates the relationship between satire and law as social instruments intended for the improvement of society through the correction of debilitating abuses. In his comedies, he condemns the false satirist, the selfish poet and the delinquent justice for perverting their professions through covetousness, ignorance, or stupidity and for thwarting virtue."

D73 Levitan, Alan L. "The Life of Our Design: The Jonsonian Masque as Baroque Form" (Princeton Univ., 1965). DA, 28 (1968), 3641-A.
"The Jonsonian masque is finally seen as a complex artistic unity in which all the contributing disciplines foster a harmonious transition from renaissance to baroque sensibility."

D74 Linden, Stanton Jay. "Alchemy and the English Literary Imagination: 1385-1633" (Univ. of Minnesota, 1971). DAI, 33 (1973), 3591-92-A.
Treats two of Jonson's works: The Alchemist and Mercury Vindicated.

D75 Linn, John G. "The Court Masque and Elizabethan Dramatic Structure, 1558-1604" (Cornell Univ., 1951).

D76 Livingston, Mary Lynda. "The Art of Jonson's Poetry" (Washington Univ., 1971). DAI, 32 (1971), 2059-A.
"This study offers a reading of Ben Jonson's poems in light of Renaissance theories of poetry and rhetoric. The method is analytic, not historical. Generalizations about Jonson's position in the history of literature are grounded in detailed analyses of the poems and illuminated by his own critical writings."

D77 Long, M. D. "Ben Jonson and Renaissance Sacralism" (Ph.D. Thesis, Cambridge, 1968-69).

D78 Lucier, James Philip. "The More Remov'd Mysteries: Neoplatonic Epistemology in the Masques of Ben Jonson" (Univ. of Michigan). DA, 24 (1963), 1162.

D79 McDonald, Elmer Milton. "John Day's Coterie Comedy" (Univ. of Virginia, 1970). DAI, 31 (1971), 4726-A.
"This work is a study of John Day's three Jacobean coterie comedies--The Ile of Guls (1606), Law-Trickes (1608) and Humour out of Breath (1608)-- in light of coterie conventions and the work of the major coterie playwrights, Jonson, Marston, and Chapman."

D80   McGinnis, Paul John.   "Integrity in the Story: A
      Study of Ben Jonson's Tragedies" (Indiana Univ.,
      1964).   DA, 25 (1964), 2984-5.

D81   McQuire, Philip C.   "'The Soul in Paraphrase': A
      Study of the Devotional Poems of Jonson, Donne,
      and Herbert." DA, 29 (1968), 1515-A.

D82   Meagher, John Carney.   "The More Removed Mys-
      teries: A Study of the Masques of Ben Jonson"
      (Princeton Univ., 1962).   DA, 23 (1963), 3381-82.

D83   Mervin, Kathleen M.   "The Development of Jonson's
      Dramatic Organization from The Case Is Altered
      through Volpone" (Cornell Univ.).   DA, 26 (1966),
      6025.

D84   Miller, Richard Henry.   "Diverse Unity: Ben Jonson's
      Epigrammes Considered Individually and Collective-
      ly" (Columbia Univ., 1972).   DAI, 33 (1972), 280-
      1-A.

D85   Mills, Lloyd Leslie.   "Ben Jonson's Last Plays: A
      Critical Reconsideration" (Univ. of Washington).
      DA, 26 (1966), 4635.

D86   Moore, Nancy Ann Newell.   "Ben Jonson's Concept of
      Decorum: A Study of his Theory and Three Come-
      dies" (Univ. of Illinois).   DA, 30 (1969), 286-A.
      The "three comedies" are Every Man In, Bar-
      tholomew Fair, and The Staple of News.

D87   Morahan, Richard Edward.   "I. Samuel Johnson and
      William Lauder's Milton Forgeries.   II. Poetry in
      Space: Disjunction in Language and Stage Action in
      Jonson's Sejanus.   III. Jane Austen's Endings"
      (Rutgers Univ., 1971).   DAI, 32 (1971), 3318-19-A.

D88   Moran, Josephine Bangs.   "The 'Recent Humors Still'
      in Jonson's Last Four Comedies" (Northwestern
      Univ.).   DA, 26 (1966), 7501.

D89   Mundhenk, Robert Thomas.   "The Jonsonian Comedy
      of Humours" (UCLA, 1971).   DAI, 32 (1971), 3262-
      63-A.

D90   Musial, Thomas James.   "The Evolution of Ben Jon-

son's Dramatic Theory: A Study in the Development
of a Moral Art" (Univ. of Notre Dame, 1970). DAI,
31 (1971), 4729-A.

D91 Nelson, Cathryn Anne. "A Critical Edition of Wit's
Triumvirate, or The Philosopher" (Univ. of Arizona).
DA, 31 (1970), 1236-A.
This play was apparently an imitation of Jonson's
The Alchemist.

D91a Nelson, Charles W. "The Insubstantial Pageant: A
Brief Examination of the Court Masque in England
with Particular Attention to Four Examples of its
Development" (Univ. of Nebraska). DAI, 32 (1971),
2650-A.
Includes a discussion of Jonson.

D92 Newton, Richard Coleman. "Foundations of Ben Jonson's Poetic Style: Epigrammes and The Forrest"
(Univ. of California, Berkeley, 1970). DAI, 32
(1971), 978-A.
Compares the "similarly theatrical" poetry of
Jonson and Martial: "Jonson, however, lacking
Martial's Emperor for an audience, possessing a
doggedly satiric trait of mind, fearing and distrust-
ing a large proportion of his readers, is much less
secure than Martial. This insecurity is at the root
of that tense defensiveness which characterizes, in
varying degrees, virtually all of Jonson's poetry."

D93 Nichols, J. G. "The Non-Dramatic Poetry of Ben
Jonson" (M. A. Thesis, University of Liverpool,
1965-66).

D94 Nichols, Mariane. "Dramatic Language in Shakespeare, Jonson and Middleton" (New York Univ.,
1971). DAI, 32 (1972), 5799-5800-A.
Deals with Epicoene and The Alchemist.

D95 Norland, Howard Bernett. "The Development of Ben
Jonson's Dramatic Technique" (Univ. of Wisconsin,
1962). DA, 23 (1962), 1352.

D96 Oates, Mary Irby. "Ben Jonson's Cary-Morison Ode:
A Critical Edition with Introduction and Commentary"
(Princeton Univ., 1972). DAI, 33 (1973), 3598-A.
"Jonson's "Cary-Morison Ode" (1629) is a major

seventeenth-century elegy that has occasioned con-
siderable critical dispute. Since it was the first
Pindaric ode to have been published in English
(and the last for another century and a half), the
unfamiliarity of the genre seems to have caused
contemporary copyists and printers some degree of
bewilderment. This confusion resulted in three
manuscripts and three early printed versions that
display substantial variations; no one is entirely
satisfactory. The 1640 folio, however, has most
authority (although printed after Jonson's death),
and I have followed all Jonson's earlier editors in
using it as copy text. "

D97   O'Dell, Jerry Clinton.   "The Influence of Poetic
Theory and Roman Comedy and Satire on Ben Jon-
son's Plays, 1596-1614" (Stanford Univ., 1972).
DAI, 33 (1972), 4357-A.

D98   Omans, Stuart E.   "The War of the Theaters: An
Approach to its Origins, Development, and Meaning" (Northwestern Univ.). DA, 30 (1970), 4951-
52-A.
Claims that the War of the Theaters "as it is
now widely understood is essentially a product of
a long and involved critical myth which was gene-
rated more by the tastes of nineteenth-century
scholars than by a discerning study of the plays
written by Ben Jonson, John Marston, and Thomas
Dekker. "

D99   Overall, Frances Morgan Bernard.   "Ben Jonson:
A Study of his Comic Theory" (Vanderbilt Univ.,
1962). DA, 23 (1962), 1352-53.

D100 Parfitt, G. A. E.   "Traditional and Original Elements in the Non-dramatic Poetry of Ben Jonson"
(Ph.D. Thesis, University of Bristol, 1966-67).

D101 Partridge, Edward B.   "The Broken Compass: A
Study of the Imagery in Ben Jonson's Comedies"
(Columbia Univ.). Microfilm Abstracts, 10 (1950),
222-23.

D102 Paster, Gail Kern.   "The Idea of the City in the
Plays, Masques, and Pageants of Ben Jonson and
Thomas Middleton" (Yale Univ., 1972). DAI, 33

(1973), 3599-A.

D103   Perry, George Francis. "A Study of the Image of
        Man in Jacobean City Comedy" (Fordham Univ.,
        1971). DAI, 32 (1971), 2067-A.
        Examples are drawn from the works of Dekker,
        Webster, Chapman, Marston, Jonson, Middleton,
        and Massinger.

D104   Peterson, Richard Scot. "The Praise of Virtue: Ben
        Jonson's Poems" (Univ. California, Berkeley).
        DA, 30 (1969), 1147-A.

D105   [no entry]

D106   Potter, L. D. "The Fop and Related Figures in
        Drama from Jonson to Cibber" (Ph. D. Thesis,
        Cambridge, Girton, 1964-65).

D107   Presley, Horton E. "'O Showes, Showes, Mighty
        Showes': A Study of the Relationship of the Jones-
        Jonson Controversy to the Rise of Illusionistic
        Staging in the Seventeenth Century British Drama"
        (Univ. of Kansas). DA, 28 (1967), 1056-A.

D108   Ransom, Shirley Farley. "Myth and Ritual in Ben
        Jonson's Earlier Dramatic Satires" (Purdue Univ.,
        1971). DAI, 32 (1972), 5199-A.
        The satires are discussed "from the viewpoint
        of their matching myth and ritual patterns--those
        of the trickster with his ritual outwitting game, the
        lord of misrule with his carnival pastimes, the
        scape goat with his expelling trial, and so on."

D109   Read, Forrest Godfrey. "Audience, Poet, and Struc-
        ture in Ben Jonson's Plays" (Cornell Univ., 1961).
        DA, 22 (1962), 3187-8.

D110   Redwine, James Daniel, Jr. "Ben Jonson's Criti-
        cism of the Drama" (Princeton Univ., 1963). DA,
        24 (1964), 4683-4.

D111   Rhome, Frances Dodson. "Variations of Festive
        Revel in Four English Comedies, 1595-1605" (In-
        diana Univ., 1969). DAI, 30 (1970), 5418-A.
        "The influences of a rustic calendar with em-
        phasis upon St. Valentine's Day and upon rural

wedding practices affect the mood of Ben Jonson's
A Tale of a Tub, considered in chapter five, in
such a way that the satirical impetus of a decadent
clergy and aristocracy is engulfed in a festive
Plough Play atmosphere. "

D112   Riddell, James Allen.   "The Evolution of the Humours Character in Seventeenth-Century English
Comedy" (Univ. of Southern California).   DA, 27
(1966), 1037-38-A.

D113   Riley, Michael Howard.   "Ritual and the Hero in
English Renaissance Tragedy" (Boston Univ., 1970).
DAI, 31 (1970), 2353-A.
This study is organized around discussions of
two plays--King Lear and Sejanus.

D114   Rivers, Isabel.   "The Poetry of Conservatism, 1600-
1745:   Jonson, Dryden, and Pope" (Columbia Univ.).
DA, 30 (1970), 4424-A.

D115   Robbins, Martin L.   "Shakespeare's Sweet Music:
A Glossary of Musical Terms in the Work of
Shakespeare (with Additional Examples from the
Plays of Lyly, Marston, and Jonson)" (Brandeis
Univ.).   DA, 30 (1969), 1534-35-A.

D116   Robinson, James Edward.   "The Dramatic Unities in
the Renaissance: A Study of the Principles, with
Application to the Development of English Drama"
(Univ. of Illinois).   DA, 20 (1959), 292.

D117   Sakowitz, Alexandre H.   "Language as Drama: Uses
of Rhetoric in Ben Jonson" (Harvard Univ.).
Summaries of Theses, 1941, 339-41.

D118   Shaw, Catherine Mand.   "The Dramatic Function of
the Masque in English Drama: 1592-1642" (Univ.
of Texas).   DA, 28 (1968), 4144-45-A.

D119   Slater, John Frederick.   "Edward Garnett: The
'Splendid Advocate; 'Volpone' and 'Antony and
Cleopatra'; The Play of Imagination; Self-Conceal-
ment and Self-Revelation in Shelley's 'Epipsychidi-
on' " (Rutgers Univ., 1971).   DAI, 32 (1971),
3332-33-A.

D120   Slights, William W. E.   "Dramatic Form in Ben Jon-
        son's Middle Comedies" (Univ. of Illinois). DA,
        27 (1967), 3881-82-A.

D121   Soule, Donald Earnest.   "Irony in Early Critical
        Comedy" (Stanford Univ.). DA, 20 (1959), 1356-7.
        Provides an analysis of Jonsonian satirical
        comedy.

D122   South, Malcolm Hudson.   "Animal Imagery in Ben
        Jonson's Plays" (Univ. of Georgia, 1968). DA, 29
        (1969), 4505-6-A.

D123   Stagg, Louis Charles.   "An Analysis and Comparison
        of the Imagery in the Tragedies of Chapman, Hey-
        wood, Jonson, Marston, Webster, Tourneur, and
        Middleton" (Univ. of Arkansas, 1963). DA, 24
        (1963), 1163-64.

D124   Stern, Charles Herman.   "Jonson's Satiric Commen-
        tator and Molière's Raisonneur: A Study Arising
        out of Parallels in Molière and Jonson" (Columbia
        Univ., 1961). DA, 22 (1962), 3188-9.

D125   Stickney, Ruth Frances.   "Formal Verse Satire from
        Lodge to Jonson, with Particular Reference to the
        Imitation of Classical Models" (Univ. of Minnesota,
        1957). DA, 17 (1957), 2017.

D126   Stodder, Joseph Henry.   "Satire in Jacobean Tragedy"
        (Univ. of Southern Calif., 1964). DA, 25 (1964),
        1898-99.
            Studies the tragedies of Marston, Jonson, and
        others.

D127   Swardson, Harold Roland, Jr.   "A Study of the Ten-
        sion between Christian and Classical Traditions in
        Seventeenth-Century Poetry" (Univ. of Minnesota,
        1956). DA, 17 (1957), 1559.

D128   Sweeney, James Gerard.   "Ben Jonson's Modern
        Literary Reputation as a Dramatist (1925-1958)"
        (Boston Univ., 1961). DA, 22 (1961), 1162-3.

D129   Targan, Barry Donald.   "Two Comic Worlds: An
        Analysis of the Structure of Thirteen of Ben Jon-
        son's Comedies" (Brandeis Univ., 1963). DA, 24

(1963), 2465.

D130   Thompson, Marvin Orville. "Uses of Music and Re-
       flections of Current Theories of the Psychology of
       Music in the Plays of Shakespeare, Jonson, and
       Beaumont and Fletcher" (Univ. of Minnesota,
       1956). DA, 16 (1956), 2448-9.

D131   Valian, Maxine Kent. "A Study of the Maturing of
       Ben Jonson's Methods of Characterization" (Univ.
       of Southern California, 1961). DA, 22 (1961), 250.

D132   Van den Berg, Sara Streich.   "The Poet in Society:
       A Study of Ben Jonson's Poetry" (Yale Univ.).
       DAI, 31 (1970), 2944-A.
       "The purpose of this dissertation is to demon-
       strate the various ways in which Ben Jonson con-
       fronts and evaluates his society through his non-
       dramatic poems. "

D133   Vawter, Marvin L. "Shakespeare and Jonson: Stoic
       Ethics and Political Crisis" (Univ. of Wisconsin).
       DA, 31 (1970), 2358-A.
       The respective authors of JC and Sejanus and
       Catiline show stoicism to be "either ineffective,
       self-defeating, paralyzing, or even deadly to a
       whole society. "

D134   Walker, Ellen Louise.   "The Varieties of Comedy:
       A Study of the Dramatic Comedies of Molière,
       Jonson and Shakespeare" (Univ. of Connecticut,
       1971). DAI, 32 (1971), 2655-A.

D135   Warr, Nancy Nairn. "The Body-Soul Debate in
       Seventeenth-Century Poetry" (Univ. of New Mexi-
       co). DA, 31 (1970), 1243-44-A.
       Discussion of the Jonsonian masque.

D136   Warren, Michael John. "The Verse Style of Ben
       Jonson's Roman Plays" (Univ. of California,
       Berkeley, 1968). DA, 30 (1969), 297-A.

D137   Weston, E. "The Poetry of Ben Jonson" (M. A. The-
       sis, University of Nottingham, England, 1956).

D138   Williams, Mary Cameron. "Unifying Methods in
       Jonson's Early Comedy" (Univ. of North Carolina,

Chapel Hill, 1970). DAI, 31 (1971), 4138-39-A.
"The purpose ... is to study the methods Ben
Jonson used to unify his early comedies from A
Tale of a Tub through Poetaster and ... to con-
sider how well his practice can be aligned with his
critical theory."

D139   Williams, Robert I.   "Skepticism in the Jacobean
       Comedies of Thomas Middleton, Ben Jonson, and
       John Fletcher" (Univ. of California, Berkeley).
       DA, 28 (1967), 207-A.

D140   Wilson, John Delane.   "Some uses of Physiognomy in
       the Plays of Shakespeare, Jonson, Marlowe, and
       Dekker" (Michigan State Univ.). DA, 26 (1966),
       4642.

D141   Witt, Robert Wayne.   "Ben Jonson and the Play-With-
       in" (Univ. of Mississippi). DAI, 31 (1970), 2894-
       A.
           Jonson "uses formal plays-within--the masque
       in Cynthia's Revels and the puppet show in Bar-
       tholomew Fair, for instance--but episodes such as
       the appearances before the Advocatori in Volpone,
       the performances of Face, Subtle, and Dol in The
       Alchemist, and the scenes before the Senate in
       Catiline, which are like plays-within and which per-
       form the same functions, are much more frequent."

D142   Young, Steven Carter.   "The Induction Plays of the
       Tudor and Stuart Drama" (Univ. of California,
       Berkeley, 1970). DAI, 32 (1971), 991-A.
           Attempts to classify types of inductions. The
       most numerous type, described as "the Extra-
       Dramatic Induction, " was largely influenced by Ben
       Jonson: Every Man Out "established its charac-
       teristic features for the next forty years. "

EDITIONS

Collected and Selected Works

E1   <u>Masques</u>, intro., testi e apparati critici, note e glossario a cura di Antonio Amato. Roma: M. Bulzoni, 1966.

E2   Bald, R. C., ed. <u>Six Elizabethan Plays</u>. Riverside Ed. Boston: Houghton Mifflin, 1963. Includes <u>Epicoene</u>.

E3   <u>Dramen, in Neudruck hrsg. nach der Folio 1616</u>, von W. Bang. 2 vols. in 1. <u>Materialien zur Kunde des älteren englischen Dramas</u>, N. S., v. 5. Louvain: A. Uystpruyst, 1905-08; Vaduz: Kraus Reprint, 1963.
        Includes <u>Every Man In</u>, <u>Every Man Out</u>, <u>Cynthia's Revels</u>, <u>Poetaster</u>, <u>Sejanus</u>, <u>Volpone</u>, <u>Epicoene</u>.

E4   Donne, John. <u>Poetry and Prose; with Izaac Walton's Life, Appreciations by Ben Jonson, Dryden, Coleridge, and Others</u>, intro. H. W. Garrod. Clarendon English Series. Oxford: Oxford Univ. Press, 1946.

E5   Duncan, Ronald, intro. <u>Poems by Ben Jonson</u>. Crown Classics. London: Grey Walls Press, 1949.

E5a   Guidi, Augusto, ed. <u>Lirica Elizabettiana</u>. Collani di Letterature Moderne, No. 12. Naples: Edizioni Scientifiche Italiane, 1960.
        An anthology from Wyatt to Jonson.

E6   Hardison, O. B., Jr., ed. <u>English Literary Criti-</u>

cism. Vol. I, The Renaissance. New York:
Appleton-Century-Crofts (Goldentree Books), 1963.
Includes "a sizable extract" from Jonson.

E7   Harrier, Richard C., ed. An Anthology of Jacobean
     Drama. Vol. I, The Stuart Editions. New York:
     New York Univ. Press, 1963.
     Includes Every Man In.

E8   Harris, Victor and Itrat Husain, eds. English Prose
     1600-1660. New York: Holt, Rinehart and Winston,
     1965.
         Selections to illustrate the capacity of 17th Cen-
     tury prose and to document some intellectual cur-
     rents; includes Jonson.

E9   Ben Jonson, ed. C. H. Herford, Percy Simpson, and
     Evelyn Simpson. Vol. IX: An Historical Survey of
     the Text, the Stage History of the Plays, and A
     Commentary on the Plays, and Vol. X: Commentary
     on the Masques. Oxford: Clarendon Press,
     1950.
         Reviewed: TLS, Jan. 12, 1951, p. 19; by W. W.
     Greg, RES, 2 (1951), 275-80 (imp.); by Henry Pop-
     kin, Theatre Arts, May 1951, pp. 2-4.

E10 Ben Jonson, ed. C. H. Herford, Percy Simpson, and
     Evelyn Simpson. Vol. XI: Jonson's Literary
     Record. Supplementary Notes. Index. Oxford:
     Clarendon Press, 1952.
         Reviewed: W. W. Greg, RES, 4 (1953), 285;
     Samuel C. Chew, N.Y. Herald Tribune Book Rev.,
     Feb. 1, 1953, p. 14; M. C. Bradbrook, MLR, 48
     (1953), 460 [brief].

E11 Ben Jonson, ed. C. H. Herford, Percy Simpson, and
     Evelyn Simpson. Vol. VIII: The Poems, The
     Prose Works. Oxford: Clarendon Press, 1947.
         Reviewed: TLS, July 5, 1947, p. 336; by W. W.
     Greg, RES, 24 (1948), 65-6; by M. C. Bradbrook,
     MLR, 43 (1948), 259-60.

E12 Hogan, Robert and Sven Eric Molin, eds. Drama:
     The Major Genres. An Introductory Critical An-
     thology. New York: Dodd, Mead & Co., 1963.
     Includes The Silent Woman.

E13   Ben Jonson, ed. John Hollander.   Laurel Poetry Series.
      New York: Dell, 1961.
      Reviewed: Wm. B. Hunter, SCN, 20 (1962), 11.

E14   The Complete Poetry of Ben Jonson, ed. William B.
      Hunter, Jr. The Stuart Editions. New York: New
      York Univ. Press, 1963; Garden City: Anchor
      Books (17th-Century Series), 1963.
      Reviewed: TLS, 1963, p. 658 [brief]; K. Wil-
      liam Fried, SCN, 21 (1963), 13.

E15   Hussey, Maurice P., ed. Jonson and The Cavaliers.
      London: Heinemann (Poetry Bookshelf), 1964.
      Includes selected poetry.

E16   Ing, Catherine, ed. Elizabethan Lyrics.   London:
      Chatto and Windus, 1951; New York: Barnes and
      Noble, 1969.

E17   Three Comedies: Volpone, The Alchemist, Bartholo-
      mew Fair, ed. Michael Jamieson. Harmondsworth:
      Penguin Books, 1966.

E18   Poems of Ben Jonson, ed. George Burke Johnston.
      The Muses' Lib. Cambridge, Mass.: Harvard
      Univ. Press, 1954; London: Routledge & Kegan
      Paul, 1954.
      Reviewed: J. I. M. Stewart, New Statesman &
      Nation, Jan. 22, 1955, pp. 110-1; TLS, May 6,
      1955, p. 236 (letters by J. C. Maxwell, June 3,
      1955, p. 301, and G. B. Johnston, June 10, 1955,
      p. 317); M. Poirier, Etudes Anglaises, 8 (1955),
      340; Hannah Buchan, RES, 7 (1956), 214-5; Her-
      mann Heuer, Shakes. Jahrbuch, 92 (1956), 364.

E19   Kenner, Hugh, ed. Seventeenth Century Poetry: The
      Schools of Donne and Jonson. New York: Holt,
      Rinehart and Winston, 1964.

E20   McPherson, David, ed. Selected Works of Ben Jon-
      son. New York: Holt, Rinehart, and Winston,
      1972.

E21   Martin, L. C., ed. The Poetical Works of Robert
      Herrick. Oxford: Oxford Univ. Press, 1956.
      Large commentary and annotations, including
      Herrick's debts to the classics and to Jonson.

E22 Muir, Kenneth, ed. Elizabethan Lyrics. A Critical
     Anthology. Life, Literature, and Thought Library.
     New York: Barnes and Noble, 1952.
     Includes five Jonson lyrics.

E23 Poems, ed. Bernard H. Newdigate. Oxford: Oxford
     Univ. Press, 1936; ed. George B. Johnston, 1954.
     Muses Library (selected).

E24 Ben Jonson, ed. and intro. Brinsley Nicholson and C.
     H. Herford. New Mermaid Series. London: Er-
     nest Benn, 1948.
        A reissue of Vol. III of the edition of 1904, with
     the essay on Jonson and the preface from Vol. I.
     Contains Volpone, Epicoene, and The Alchemist.

E25 Ben Jonson, ed. and intro., Brinsley Nicholson and C.
     H. Herford. New York: A. A. Wyn, 1948.
        Contains Epicoene, Volpone, and The Alchemist.
     Formerly published in Mermaid Series in 3 volumes.
     This is original Vol. III but includes the essay on
     Jonson and the preface from Vol. I.

E26 Nicholson, Brinsley, and C. H. Herford, eds. Ben
     Jonson (Three Plays). With intro. and notes. A
     Mermaid Dramabook. New York: Hill and Wang,
     1957.

E27 The Complete Masques, ed. Stephen Orgel. The Yale
     Ben Jonson. New Haven: Yale Univ. Press, 1969.

E28 Ben Jonson: Selected Masques, ed. Stephen Orgel.
     The Yale Ben Jonson, Vol. 4, abridged. New
     Haven: Yale Univ. Press, 1970.
        Selected from Orgel's The Complete Masques.

E29 Ornstein, Robert, and Hazelton Spencer, eds. Eliza-
     bethan and Jacobean Comedy: An Anthology. Bos-
     ton: D. C. Heath, 1964.
        Includes Every Man In His Humor and The Al-
     chemist.
        Reviewed: J. E. Parsons, SCN, 22.3-4 (1964),
     44.

E29a Partridge, A. C., ed. The Tribe of Ben: Pre-
     Augustan Classical Verse in England. Arnold's
     English Texts. London: Edward Arnold, 1966.

E30   Praz, Mario, ed. Teatro Elisabettiano: Kyd, Mar-
       lowe, Heywood, Marston, Jonson, Webster, Tour-
       neur, Ford. Florence: Sansoni, 1948.
       Reviewed: Allardyce Nicoll, MLR, 44 (1949),
       261-2.

E31   Redwine, James D., Jr., ed. Ben Jonson's Literary
       Criticism. Regents Critics Series. Lincoln: Univ.
       of Nebraska Press, 1970.

E32   Sabol, Andrew J., ed. A Score for Lovers Made Men,
       a Masque by Ben Jonson. The music adapted and
       arranged for composition by Nicholas Lanier, Al-
       phonso Ferrabosco, and their contemporaries.
       Providence: Brown Univ. Press, 1963.
       Reviewed: Stanley Wells, MLR, 49 (1964), 107;
       Stoddard Lincoln, Theatre Notebook, 18 (1964), 68-
       69; Mortimer H. Frank, SCN, 22 (1964), 51; F. W.
       Sternfeld, RES, 14 (1963), 409-10; Chalmers Burns,
       NSQ, n. s. 12 (1965), 159.

E33   Sabol, Andrew J., ed. Songs and Dances for the
       Stuart Masque. Providence: Brown Univ. Press,
       1959.

E34   Five Plays, ed. F. E. Schelling. World's Classics.
       London and New York: Oxford Univ. Press, 1953.
       Includes: Every Man In His Humour, Sejanus,
       Volpone, The Alchemist, and Bartholomew Fair.

E35   Spencer, T. J. B., et al, ed. A Book of Masques:
       In Honor of Allardyce Nicoll. London: Cambridge
       Univ. Press, 1967.
       Includes Pleasure Reconciled to Virtue, Lovers
       Made Men, and Love Freed from Ignorance and
       Folly.

E35a   Stroup, Thomas B., ed. The Selected Poems of
       George Daniel of Beswick, 1616-1657. Lexington:
       Kentucky Univ. Press, 1959.
       Daniel "looks back to Spenser and Samuel Daniel,
       and the gods of his adoration are Jonson, Donne,
       and Herbert. "

E36   White, Helen C., Ruth C. Wallerstein, and Ricardo
       Quintana, eds. Seventeenth-Century Verse and
       Prose, Volume One: 1600-1660. New York:
       Macmillan, 1951.

Individual Works: Editions, Adaptations, Translations,
Textual Commentaries

A. JONSON'S PROSE

E37 Discoveries, 1641. Conversations with William Drum-
      mond of Hawthornden, 1619. Edinburgh: Edinburgh
      Univ. Press, 1966.
          Reprint of the first edition published in 1923.

E38 Gollancz, Israel, ed. Timber: Or, Discoveries:
      Made upon Men and Matter. Temple Classics. Re-
      print edition. London: J. M. Dent, 1951.

E39 Harrison, G. B., ed. Discoveries, 1641. Conversa-
      tions with William Drummond of Hawthornden, 1619.
      New York: Barnes & Noble, 1966.

E40 Ben Jonson's Timber or Discoveries, ed. Ralph S.
      Walker. Syracuse, N.Y.: Syracuse Univ. Press,
      1953.
          Reviewed: J. C. Bryce, Aberdeen Univ. Rev.,
      36 (1955), 189-90.

B. JONSON'S MASQUES AND PLAYS

E41 Cole, George Watson, ed. The Gypsies Metamorphosed.
      A Variorum edition. New York: Kraus Reprint,
      1966.

E42 Pleasure Reconciled to Virtue, ed. R. A. Foakes in
      A Book of Masques: In Honor of Allardyce Nicoll,
      ed. T. J. B. Spencer, et al. London: Cambridge
      Univ. Press, 1967, pp. 225-50.

E43 Jonson's Masque of Gipsies in The Burley, Belvoir,
      and Windsor Versions. An Attempt at a Recon-
      struction by W. W. Greg. London: Oxford Univ.
      Press for British Academy, 1952.
          Reviewed: Fredson Bowers, RES, 4 (1953),
      172-7; Harold Jenkins, MLR, 48 (1953), 70-3.

E44 Oberon, the Fairy Prince, ed. Richard Hosley, in A
      Book of Masques: In Honor of Allarydyce Nicoll,
      ed. T. J. B. Spencer, et al. London: Cambridge
      Univ. Press, 1967, pp. 43-70.

E45   Jump, J. D., ed. Rollo Duke of Normandy, or the
Bloody Brother: A Tragedy Attributed to John
Fletcher, George Chapman, Ben Jonson and Philip
Massinger. Liverpool English Text and Studies.
Liverpool: Univ. of Liverpool Press, 1948.
Reviewed: A. M. P., Manchester Guard. Week-
ly, March 10, 1949, p. 13; N&Q, 194 (1949), 264;
H. Jenkins, MLR, 44 (1949), 563-4; C. Leech, RES,
N. Ser. I (1950), 360-2; J. E. Savage, MLN,
65 (1950), 564-5; E. M. Waith, MLQ, 11 (1950),
499-500.

E46   Love Freed From Ignorance and Folly, ed. Norman
Sandlers, in A Book of Masques: In Honor of Allardyce Nicoll, ed. T. J. B. Spencer, et al. London: Cambridge Univ. Press, 1967, pp. 71-93.

E47   Lovers Made Men, ed. Stanley Wells, in A Book of
Masques: In Honor of Allardyce Nicoll, ed. T. J.
B. Spencer, et al. London: Cambridge Univ.
Press, 1967, pp. 207-23.

E48   The Alchemist. London 1612. The English Experience, No. 330. Amsterdam: Theatrum Orbis Terrarum, 1971 [Reprint].

E49   The Alchemist, ed. J. B. Bamborough. London:
Macmillan, 1967; New York: St. Martins, 1967.

E50   The Alchemist, ed. G. E. Bentley. New York:
Crofts Classics, 1947.

E51   The Alchemist, ed. Douglas Brown. The New Mermaids. London: Benn, 1966.
Reviewed: G. R. Proudfoot, N&Q, 212 (1967),
356-60.

E52   The Alchemist, ed. from the Quarto of 1612, with
comments on its text by Henry de Vocht. Materials
for the Study of The Old English Drama, N.S., V.
22. Louvain: Uystpruyst, 1950.

E53   The Alchemist, ed. John I. McCollum, Jr. Woodbury,
N.Y.: Barron's Educational Series, 1965.

E54   The Alchemist, ed. Francis H. Mares. The Revels
Plays. London: Methuen, 1967; Cambridge, Mass.:

Harvard Univ. Press, 1967.

E55 L'alchimiste; comedie en cinq actes. Adaptation de
     Marcel Moussy. Paris: L'Anche; Lausanne: La
     Cite, 1962.

E56 The Alchemist, ed. Sidney Musgrove. Fountainwell
     Drama Texts. Edinburgh: Oliver and Boyd, 1968;
     Berkeley: Univ. of Cal. Press, 1968.

E57 The Alchemist: Testo riveduto, versione integrale a
     fronte in versi, prefazione, introduzione e note. A
     cura di A. Obertello. Florence: Sansoni, 1948.

E58 The Alchemist, ed. Arthur Sale. London: Univ. Tu-
     torial Press, 1969.

E59 The Alchemist, ed. J. B. Steane. London: Cam-
     bridge Univ. Press, 1967.

E60 Bartholomew Fair, ed. E. A. Horsman. Revels Plays.
     London: Methuen, 1960; Cambridge, Mass.: Har-
     vard Univ. Press, 1960.
         Reviewed: Kenneth Palmer, MLR, 56 (1961),
     584; C. L. Barber, AUMLA, No. 16 (1962), pp.
     202-3; J. B. Bambrough, RES, 14 (1963), 197-8.

E61 Bartholomew Fair, ed. Maurice P. Hussey. New Mer-
     maid Series. London: Ernest Benn, 1964.
         Reviewed: Fernand Largarde, Etudes Anglaises,
     18 (1965), 179-80.

E62 Bartholomew Fair, ed. Edward B. Partridge. Re-
     gents Renaissance Drama Series. Lincoln: Univ.
     of Nebraska Press, 1964.
         Reviewed: Ian Donaldson, Essays In Criticism,
     15 (1965), 453-8; A. A., Personalist, 50 (1965),
     57-8; Jack W. Jesse, SCN, 23.1-2, 4, 6 (1965);
     Norman Sanders, MLR, 61 (1966), 279-81.

E63 Bartholomew Fair, ed. Eugene M. Waith. The Yale
     Ben Jonson. New Haven: Yale Univ. Press, 1963.
         Reviewed: Matthew N. Proser, SCN, 22.1
     (1964), 10-11.

E64 The Fountaine of Self-love; or, Cynthia's Revels.
     Nach der quarto 1601 in neudruck hrsg. Von W.

Bang und L. Krebs. Materialien zur Kunde des
älteren englischen Dramas, N. S., Vol. 11. Louvain: A. Uystpruyst, 1908; Vaduz: Kraus Reprint,
1963.

E65 [no entry]

E66 The Divell is an Asse, ed. Maurice Hussey. London:
Univ. Tutorial Press, 1967.

E67 Epicoene; or, The Silent Woman, ed. L. A. Beaurline.
Regents Renaissance Drama Series. Lincoln: Univ.
of Nebraska Press, 1966; London: E. Arnold, 1967.
Reviewed: Mary Mahl, Personalist, 48 (1967),
425.

E68 Epicoene, ed. Edward Partridge. The Yale Ben Jonson. New Haven: Yale Univ. Press, 1971.

E69 Every Man in His Humour, A Comedy, in Five Acts,
by Ben Jonson. Printed from the acting copy, with
remarks.... As performed Theatres Royal, London.... London: G. H. Davidson, n. d.

E70 Every Man in His Humor, Reprinted from The Quarto
1601 by W. Bang and W. W. Greg. Materialien
zur Kunde des älteren englischen Dramas, N. S.,
Vol. 4. Louvain: A. Uystpruyst, 1905; Vaduz:
Kraus Reprint, 1963.

E71 Every Man in His Humor, ed. Gabriele Bernhard Jackson. The Yale Ben Jonson. New Haven: Yale Univ.
Press, 1969.

E72 Every Man in His Humour, ed. R. S. Knox. 2nd ed.
London: Methuen and Co., 1965.

E73 Every Man in His Humour; A Parallel-Text Edition of
the 1601 Quarto and the 1616 Folio, ed. J. W.
Lever. Regents Renaissance Drama Series. Lincoln: Univ. of Nebraska Press, 1971.

E74 Every Man in His Humour, ed. Arthur Sale. 3rd
Rev. ed. London: Univ. Tutorial Press, 1968.

E75 Every Man in His Humor, ed. M. Seymour-Smith.
The New Mermaids. London: Ernest Benn, 1966;

New York: Hill and Wang, 1968.
Reviewed: G. R. Proudfoot, N&Q, 213 (1968),
154-5.

E76 Every Man Out of His Humour, Reprinted from
Holme's Quarto of 1600, ed. W. Bang and W. W.
Greg. Materialien zur Kunde des älteren englischen
Dramas, N. S. , Vol. 7. Louvain: A. Uystpruyst;
Vaduz: Kraus Reprint, 1963.

E77 Every Man Out of His Humor, Reprinted from Linge's
Quarto of 1600, ed. by W. Bang and W. W. Greg.
Materialien zur Kunde des älteren englischen
Dramas, Vol. 17. Louvain: A. Uystpruyst, 1907;
Vaduz: Kraus Reprint, 1963.

E78 de Vocht, Henry, ed. Ben Jonson's Poetaster; or,
The Arraignment, edited from The Quarto of 1602
by Henry de Vocht. Materials for the Study of the
Old English Drama, N. S. , Vol. 9. Louvain: Li-
braire Universitaire, C. Uystpruyst, 1934; Vaduz:
Kraus Reprint, 1965.

E79 Sad Shepherd. With Waldron's Continuation, ed. W.
W. Greg. Materialien zur Kunde des älteren
englischen Dramas, N. S. , Vol. 4. Louvain:
Uystpruyst, 1905; Vaduz: Kraus, 1963.

E80 Sejanus, His Fall. London, 1605. The English Experience, No. 265. Amsterdam: Theatrum Orbis
Terrarum, 1970 [Reprint].

E81 Sejanus, ed. Jonas A. Barish. The Yale Ben Jon-
son. New Haven: Yale Univ. Press, 1965.
Reviewed: David Novarr, ELN, 4 (1966), 65-8;
G. R. Hibbard, MLR, 61 (1966), 672-3; James E.
Robinson, SCN, 24 (1966), 10-11; G. R. Proudfoot,
N&Q, 212 (1967), 356-60.

E82 Sejanus His Fall, ed. W. F. Bolton. The New Mermaids. London: Ernest Benn, 1966; New York:
Hill and Wang, 1969.
Reviewed: G. R. Proudfoot, N&Q, 212 (1967),
356-60.

E83 Seianus his Fall. Edited from The Quarto of 1605
with Comments on its Text by Henry de Vocht.

Materials for the Study of the Old English Drama,
N.S., Vol. 11. Louvain: Libraire Universitaire,
C. Uystpruyst, 1935; Vaduz: Kraus Reprint, 1963.

E84 [no entry]

E85 A Tale of a Tub, nach dem Drucke von 1640, hrsg.
von Hans Scherer. Materialien zur Kunde des
älteren englischen Drama, N.S., Vol. 17. Louvain:
A. Uypstpruyst, 1913; Vaduz: Kraus, 1963.

E86 Volpone: 1607. Menston: Scolar Press, 1968. A
facsimile of the edition of 1607.

E87 Volpone; or, The Fox, ed. with an introd. and notes
by J. B. Bamborough. English Classics, New
Series. London: Macmillan, 1964.

E88 Volpone, ed. Jonas A. Barish. New York: Crofts
Classics, 1958.
Reviewed: George E. Nichols, III, CE, 22
(1960), 56.

E89 Volpone, ed. Philip Brockbank. The New Mermaids.
London: Benn, 1968; New York: Hill and Wang,
1969.

E90 Ben Jonson: Volpone. The Alchemist, ed. Janet
Brunoski. New York: Barnes and Noble, 1970.

E91 Volpone ou le Renard. Texte établi par. M. Chaste-
lain. Paris: Belles-Lettres, 1946.

E92 Volpone, ed. David Cook. Methuen's English Classics.
London: Methuen, 1962.
Reviewed: N. W. Bawcutt, MLR, 58 (1963),
315-6.

E93 Volpone; or, The Fox, ed. David Cook. New York:
Barnes and Noble, 1967; London: Methuen & Co.,
1967 [Paper].

E94 Volpone; or, The Foxe. Edited from the Quarto of
1607, with Comments on its Text by Henry de
Vocht. Materials for the Study of the Old English
Drama, N.S., Vol. 13. Louvain: Libraire Universitaire, C. Uystpruyst, 1937; Vaduz: Kraus, 1963.

E95   Volpone, ed. J. L. Halio. Fountainwell Drama
       Texts. Berkeley: Univ. of Cal. Press, 1968;
       Edinburgh: Oliver & Boyd, 1968.

E96   Volpone, or The Fox, ed. Vincent F. Hopper and
       Gerald B. Lahey, with a note on the staging by
       George L. Hersey. Great Neck, N.Y.: Barron's,
       1959.

E97   Volpone, ed. Alvin B. Kernan. The Yale Ben Jon-
       son. New Haven: Yale Univ. Press, 1962.

E98   Ben Jonson: Volpone, ed. Alvin B. Kernan. New
       Haven: Yale Univ. Press, 1964 [Paper].
       Reviewed: SCN, 21 (1963), 23 [brief]; Edward
       B. Partridge, RN, 17.1 (1964), 21-3; C. G.
       Thayer, BA, 38.2 (1964), 189.

E99   Volpone, intro. Louis Kronenberger. Printed for the
       members of the Limited Editions Club: Oxford,
       1952. Illustrations by René Ben Sussan.

E100   Volpone; or, The Fox, intro. Henry G. Lee. San
       Francisco: Chandler Pub. Co., 1961.

E101   Volpone. Testo riveduto con versione a fronte, in-
       troduzione e note a cura di Mario Praz. Biblio-
       teca Sansoniana Straniera, No. 83. Firenze:
       Sansoni, 1943.

E102   Volpone, d'après Ben Jonson; Par Jules Romains et
       Stefan Zweig. Paris: Gallimard, 1965.
       "Volpone a été representé pour la première
       fois à Paris le 23 Novembre 1928."

E103   Volpone, or the Fox, ed. Arthur Sale. London:
       Univ. Tutorial Press, 1951.

E104   Volpone. Adaptación de Rafael Tasis. Palma de
       Mallorca: Editorial Moll, 1957.

E105   Volpone, ed. and intro. Louis B. Wright and Vir-
       ginia A. LaMar. New York: Washington Square
       Press, 1970.

E106   Zweig, S. Ben Jonsons "Volpone." Eine lieblose
       Komödie in drei Akten. Frankfurt am Main, 1950.

Note that this German adaptation is described
as "Eine freie Umformung des Textes."

INDEX

of Names and Subjects

The Alchemist A8, A37,
A109, A113, A125, A141,
A180, A203, A216, A217,
A228, A244, A256, A264,
A268, A337, A350, A375,
A394, A413, A433, B7,
B15, B57, B58, B71, B74,
B124, B133, B136, B158,
D36, D37, D74, D91, D94,
D141, E17, E24, E29,
E34, E48-E59
Allegory A126
Allen, Frank A1
Allen, Richard O. D1
Amato, Antonio E1
Anderson, Donald K. A2
Anderson, Mark A. A3, D2
Antimasque A157
Arden, John A5
Aristophanes B63, D52,
D69
Armstrong, Wm. A. A6
Arnold, Hans Stephan D3
Arnold, Judd Baldwin A7,
A8, D4
Arnstein, Robt. A9
Ashton, Robt. A10
Asthana, R. K. B1
Atkins, J. W. H. B2
Aylward, J. D. A11, A12

Babb, Howard S. A13

Babb, Lawrence B3
Babington, Bruce A14
Bachrach, A. G. H. A15
Bacon, Francis A357, B27,
B45, B48, B134
Bacon, Wallace A. A16
Bald, R. C. E2
Baldini, Gabriele B4
Balestri, Charles Angelo D5
Bamborough, J. B. A17,
A18, B5, B6, E49, E87
Bang, W. E3, E64, E70,
E76, E77
Barber, C. L. B7
Barish, Jonas A. A19, A20,
A21, A22, A304, B8-B10,
E81, E88
Barker, J. R. A23
Barker, Walter L. D6
Barnes, Peter A24
Barr, C. B. L. A25
Bartholomew Fair A22, A86,
A232, A250, A253, A260,
A264, A287, A323, A336,
A349, A355, A370, A384,
A429, A432, A445, A446,
B14, B15, B38, B59, B71,
B104, B133, B169, D32,
D36, D43, D60, D86,
D141, E17, E34, E60-E63
Bauer, Robert V. D7
Baum, Helena Watts B11
Beaumont, Francis A170,

153

A212, A213, A395, A400,
B173, D3, D130
Beaurline, L. A.   A26, A27,
E67
Benham, Allen R.   A28
Benn, C. De C. W.   D8
Bennett, J. W.   A29, A30,
B165
Bentley, G. E.   B12-B14,
E50
Bergeron, David M.   A31
Bergman, Jos. A.   A32
Berlin, Normand   B15
Berry, Herbert   A33
Bevington, David   B15a
Bishop, David H.   A34
Black, Matthew   B16
Blanshard, Rufus A.   A35,
B17
Blissett, Wm.   A36, A37
Bluestone, Max   B17a
Blunden, Edmund   A38
Boas, F. S.   A39, B18
Bocan, Sister Agnes   D9
Boddy, Margaret   A40
Bolton, W. F.   E82
Boughner, Daniel C.   A42-
A47, B19, B20
Boyd, John D.   A48
Bradbrook, F. W.   A49
Bradbrook, M. C.   B21
Bredvold, Louis I.   A50
Brock, Dewey Heyward   D10
Brockbank, Philip   E89
Brome, Richard   B30
Brooks, Cleanth   B22
Brooks, Harold F.   A51
Brown, A. D. F.   A52
Brown, Arthur   A53
Brown, Douglas   E51
Brown, Huntington   B23
Brown, Ivor   A54
Browne, William   A97, D20
Brunoski, Janet   E90
Bryant, Jos. A., Jr.   A55-
A60, B24
Bullett, Gerald   A61

Burke, George   E18
Burke-Severs, J.   A62
Burns, Robert Lee   D11
Burton, K. M.   A63
Bush, Douglas   B25
Buxton, John   A64

Cable, Chester H.   A65
Cain, Thomas Henry   D12
Calder, Daniel G.   A66
Caldiero, Frank   A67
Camden, Carroll   A68
Camden, Wm.   A156
Campbell, Marian Selma John-
son   D13
Campbell, O. J.   B137
Campion, Th.   A348
Cannon, Chas. K.   A69
Capone, Giovanna   B26
Carew, Th.   A35, A310,
A332, B17
Carpenter, Chas. A.   A70
Case is Altered, The   A133,
A215, A319, D83
Castelain, M.   E91
Castle, Edward J.   B27
Catiline   A57, A65, A118,
A122, A127, A200, A283,
A449, B34, D30, D50,
D133, D141
Celia   A52, A424, A441
Chalfant, Fran Cernocky   D14
Champion, Larry Stephen
A71, A72, B28, D15
Chan, Mary   A73
Chapman, George   A2, A63,
A181, A199, A212, A237,
A396, A439, B108, B122,
B145, B151, D1, D71,
D79, D103, D123, E45
Chapman, Mildred Shows
D16
Chaucer, Geof.   A277, A323
Child, Harold   B139
Chloridia   A175
Christopher, Georgia B.   D17

154

Chute, Marchette B29
Clancy, James H. A74
Clary, F. N. A75
Clausen, Wendell A76
Clearman, Mary Rebecca
  Hogeland D18
Cloudsley, Annabella A77
Clubb, Roger Lane A78,
  D19
Cohen, Gerald D20
Coiseault-Cavalea, M. A79
Cole, George Watson E41
Combellack, F. M. A80
Comedy of manners D13
Commedia dell'arte D6
Cone, Mary D21
Connor, Rodney Vincent
  D22
Cook, David E92, E93
Cook, E. B30, D23
Cookman, A. V. A81
Cope, Jackson I. A82-A86
Cornelia, Sister M. Bona-
  venture D24
Coterie drama D1, D79
Couillard, Theophane Venard
  D25
Court D16
Cox, Gerald H., III A87
Craik, T. W. A88
Criticism B2, B85, B86,
  B90, B134, B135, B141,
  B144, B152, B174, D44,
  D56, D99, D110, E6,
  E10, E31
Cross, Gustav A89
Crupi, Charles William D26
Cubeta, Paul M. A90-A92,
  D27
Cunningham, Delora A93
Cunningham, J. E. B31
Currey, R. N. A94
Curry, Rev. John Vincent
  B32, D28
Cutts, John P. A95-A103
Cynthia's Revels A73, A139,
  A356, A376, A377, A436,
B36a, D141, E3, E64

Dale, Leona Ford A105, D29
Danby, John F. A106
Davis, Joe Lee B33
Davis, Tom A107
Davison, Peter H. A108
Dawson, G. E. B166
Day, John D79
Deception D28, D43, D67
Decorum D86
Dekker, Thomas A31, A453a,
  B110, D98, D103, D140
DeLuna, Barbara B34, D30
Demaray, John G. B35, D31
Denniston, Elliott Averett
  D32
DeSante, Rev. Paul John
  D33
Dessen, Alan Charles A109-
  A111, B36, D34
DeVilliers, Jacob I. A112
deVocht, Henry B36a, B36b,
  E52, E78, E83, E94
Dircks, Richard J. A113
Discoveries A66, A209,
  A278, A403, A448, A457,
  B178, E37-E40
Divell is an Asse A365,
  A383, A391, A440, B15,
  B136, E66
Dobbs, Leonard B37
Donaldson, Ian A114-A117
  B38
Donne, John A49, A80, A90,
  A91, A310, A423, A454,
  B17, B25, B81, B97, B99,
  B100, B111, B120, D81,
  E4
Doolittle, Hilda B39
Doran, Madeleine B40
Dorenkamp, Angela G. A118
Doughtie, Edward A119
Douglass, James W. A120
Dowling, Linda Crabill D35
Drama A53, A152, A171,

A233, A236, A270, A291,
A345, A358, B77, D57,
D58, D94, D95, D98,
D106, D116, E9, E26
Draper, R. P. A121
Drayton, Michael A339,
B106
Drew-Bear, Annette D36
Drummond, William, of
Hawthornden A23, A162,
A289, A447, E37, E38
Dryden, John A153, A465,
B22, B134
Dudley, Leonea Barbour
D37
Duffy, Ellen M. T. A122
Duncan, Douglas A123,
A124
Duncan, Edgar Hill A125
Duncan, Ronald E5
Dunlap, Rhodes A126
Dunn, Esther C. B41

Earley, Robert Schafer D38
Eastward Ho! A82, A208,
A347, A397
Echeruo, Michael J. C.
A127
Ekeblad, Inga-Stina A128
Elegy A307, D63
Eliot, T. S. A48
Elton, Wm. A129
Empson, Wm. A130
Emslie, MacDonald A131,
A132
Enck, John J. A133, A134,
B42, D39
English, Hubert M., Jr.
D40
Enright, D. J. A135, A136,
B43
Epicoene A3, A20, A70,
A104, A114, A144, A245,
A301, A342, A375, A381,
A387, A406, B38, B49,
B59, B62, B71, B133,

B136, D59, D94, E2, E3,
E12, E24, E67, E68
Epigrammes A143, A222,
A227, A276, A305, A320,
A359, A464, D38, D61,
D70, D84, D92
Evans, K. W. A137, D41
Evans, Maurice B44
Everett, Barbara A138
Every Man In His Humour
A11, A58, A202, A258,
A280, A295, A371, B71,
B95, D71, D86, E3, E7,
E29, E34, E69-E75
Every Man Out of His Humour
A59, A161, A214, A285,
A290, A375, A409, A452,
B32, B95, D19, D71,
D142, E3, E76, E77

Fabian, B. A139
Farmer, Norman K., Jr.
A140
Feather, John A141
Fellowes, Peter A143
Ferns, John A144
Field, Michael Jay D42
Field, Nathan A346, A347
Fieler, Frank B. B45
Fike, Francis A145
Fisher, Wm. N. A146
Fletcher, John A170, A212,
A213, A437, B173, D3,
D20, D21, D130, D139,
E45
Flower, Annette Chappell
D43
Foakes, R. A. E42
Ford, John A261, E30·
Forrest A84, D92
Fox, Robert C. A148
Frajnd, Marta A149
Fraser, P. M. B46
Fredeman, Patsy Dale Hines
D44
Freehafer, John A150

156

Freeman, Arthur A151
Freeman, R. D45
French, John T. A152
Fricker, Franz B47
Fried, Gisela A153
Friedman, Wm. F. and
Elizabeth S. B48
Friedson, Anthony M. B49
Frost, David A154
Frye, Northrop B51, B52
Furniss, Warren Todd
A155-A157, B50, D46

Gagen, Jean B53
Galloway, David B149
Gardiner, Judith Kegan
D47
Gardner, Th. B54
Gassner, John B133
George A. G. B134
Gerritsen, Johan A158
Gianakaris, Constantine
John A159, D48
Gibbons, Brian B55
Gibson, C. A. A160
Gilbert, Allan H. A161-
A163, B56, B57
Goldberg, S. L. A164
Goldsmith, Robt. H. A165
Gollancz, Israel E38
Gombosi, Otto A166
Goodman, Paul B58
Gordon, D. J. A167-A169
Gossett, Suzanne A170
Gottwald, M. A171, A172,
B59, D49
Graham, Hugh R. D50
Gray, Henry David A173,
A174
Graziani, R. I. C. A175
Greene, Robt. B27, B114
Greene, Th. M. A176,
A177
Greg, W. W. A178, B60-
B62, E43, E70, E76,
E77, E79

Grow, Gerald O. D51
Guidi, Augusto E5a
Gum, Coburn B63, D52
Gunby, D. C. A179
Gypsies Metamorphosed E41

Haddington Masque A168
Hahamovitch, Lillian D53
Halio, J. L. A181, E95
Hallett, Chas. A. A182-
A184
Halliday, F. E. B64
Hamilton, Gary D. A185
Hammood, Emily Evans D54
Han, Pierre A186
Hardison, O. B., Jr. B65,
E6
Harrier, Richard C. E7
Harris, Victor A187, E8
Harrison, G. B. E39
Hart, Jeffrey A188
Hartman, Jay H. A189
Hawkins, Harriet B. A190-
A192, D55
Haworth, W. D56
Hayashi, Tetsumaro A193
Hays, H. R. A194
Heffner, Ray L., Jr. A195,
B66, B85
Heinsius, Daniel B152
Held, Geo. A196
Hemphill, Geo. A197, B67
Heninger, S. K., Jr. B68
Henke, James Thomas D57
Herbert, George A91, A310,
B111, D81
Herford, C. H. E9-E11,
E24-E26
Herrick, Marvin T. B69
Herrick, Robt. A240, A296,
B106, E21
Hersey, George L. E96
Heywood, Thomas D123
Hibbard, G. R. A198, A199
Hill, Geoffrey A200
Hoffman, Gerhard A201

157

Hogan, Robert E12
Holden, William P.   B70
Hollander, John   A202, E13
Holleran, James V.   A203
Hollway, Morag   A204
Holt, Albert Hamilton   D58
Holzknecht, Karl J.   B71
Honesty   D60
Honig, Edwin   A205, A206
Hopper, Vincent F.   E96
Horace   A28, A44, D66
Horn, Robt. D.   A207
Horsman, E. A.   E60
Horwich, Richard   A208
Hosley, Richard   E44
Houck, Joseph Kemp   A209,
   D59
Houser, David John   D60
Howarth, Herbert   A210,
   A211, B72
Howarth, R. G.   B73
Hoy, Cyrus   A212, A213,
   B74
Humanism   B107, D48
Humez, Jean McMahon   D61
Humours   A74, A133, A172,
   A247, A364, A408, A421,
   A430, D7, D66, D88,
   D89, D112
Hunt, Effie N.   D62
Hunter, G. K.   A214
Hunter, William B., Jr.
   E14
Huntley, Frank L.   A215
Husain, Itrat   E8
Hussey, Maurice P.   A216,
   A217, E15, E61, E66
Hutchison, Barbara   A218
Huygens, Sir Constantyn
   A15
Hyde, Mary Crapo   B75
Hymenaei   A85, A128, A167,
   A316

Imagery   A344, A411, B127,
   D39, D101, D103, D122,

D123
Ing, Catherine   E16
Inglis, Fred   A219, B76
Irony   A123, A185

Jackson, Gabriele Bernhard
   B77, E71
Jamieson, Michael   E17
Janicka, Irena   A220, A221
Jayne, Sears   B78
Johansson, Bertil   B79, B80
John, Lisle Cecil   A222,
   A223
Johnson, Carol Holmes   B81
Johnson, Nell E.   D63
Johnson, Robert   A101
Johnston, Elizabeth Carring-
   ton   D64
Johnston, Geo. B.   A224-
   A227, B82, E23
Jones, Inigo   A103, A169,
   A324, A431, B83, D8,
   D107
Jones, Myrddin   A228
Jones, Robert Charles   A229,
   D65
Jones-Davies, M. Th.   B83
Jonsonius Virbius   A210
Joyce, James   A18, B72
Jump, J. D.   E45
Jungnell, Tore   A231, B84
Justice   A257, A258, D72
Juvenal   A20, A46, A144,
   A274, D18

Kaplan, Joel H.   A232
Kaufmann, R. J.   B85
Kay, W. David   A233, A234,
   D66
Keast, W. R.   A235, B86,
   B96, B174
Kennedy, Dennis Edward
   D67
Kennedy-Skipton, A. L. D.
   A236

Kenner, Hugh E19
Kermode, J. F. A237
Kernan, Alvin B. B87, B88,
  E97, E98
Kifer, Devra Rowland A238
Kim, Seyong A239
Kirby, Th. A. A240, A241
Kirchner, Gustav A242
Kirsch, Arthur A. B88a
Kirschbaum, Leo B89
Klein, David B90
Kliegman, Benjamine A243
Knights, L. C. B85, B91,
  B92
Knoll, Robt. E. A244, B93
Knox, R. S. E74
Kranidas, Th. A245
Krebs, L. E64
Krishnamurthi, M. G.
  A246
Krishnappa, Josephine Bala-
  mani D68
Kronenberger, Louis B94,
  E99
Kyd, Thomas A69, A420,
  B16, B114, D45, E30

Lafkidou, Aliki D69
LaFrance, Marston A247
Lahey, Gerald B. E96
LaMar, Virginia A. B183,
  E105
Langsam, G. Geoffrey B95
Language A231, A334,
  A340, B8, B84, B126,
  B128, B129, B142, B143,
  B159
Langvardt, Arthur LeRoy
  D70
LaRegina, Gabriella A248
Lascelles, Mary A249
Late plays B28, D15, D85
Latham, Jacqueline E. M.
  A250
Lavin, J. A. A251
Law, Richard A. A252

Lawson, Anita Saffels D71
Leavis, F. R. B96
LeComte, Edward B97
Lee, Henry G. E100
Lee, Umphrey A253
Leech, Clifford B98
Leggatt, Alexander A254
Leishman, J. B. B99, B100
Lemay, J. A. Leo A255
Lever, J. W. E73
Levin, Harry A256, B101
Levin, Lawrence Lee A257,
  A258, D72
Levin, Richard A259-A264
Levitan, Alan L. D73
Linden, Stanton Jay D74
Lindsay, Barbara N. A265
Linn, John G. D75
Litt, Dorothy E. A266
Livingston, Mary Lynda D76
Lodge, Oliver A267
London D14
Long, M. D. D77
Love banquet A2
Love Freed from Ignorance
  and Folly E35, E46
Lovers Made Men E32, E35,
  E47
Love's Welcome at Bolsover
  A102
Lucier, James Philip D78
Lyly, John B114, D115

MacCarthy, Desmond B103
McCollom, Wm. G. B104
McCollum, John I., Jr.
  E53
McCullen, Jos. T., Jr.
  A268
McCutcheon, Elizabeth A269
McDiarmid, Matthew P.
  A270
McDonald, Chas. O. A271
McDonald, Elmer Milton
  D79
McElroy, David D. A272

McEuen, Kathryn A.   A274
McFarland, Ronald E.
   A275, A276
McGalliard, John C.   A277
McGinnis, Paul John   A278,
   A279, D80
McGlinchee, Claire   A280
Machiavelli, N.   A45, B20,
   B131, B163
McKenzie, D. F.   A281
McKenzie, James   A282
Mackin, Cooper R.   A283
Maclean, Hugh   B105
McManaway, J. G.   B166
McMillin, Scott   A284
McNeal, Th. H.   A285
McPherson, David   A286,
   E20
McQuire, Philip C.   D81
Maddison, Carol   B106
Mager, Don   A287
Magnetic Lady, The   A72,
   A83, A275, A323
Main, C. F.   A288, A289
Main, Wm. W.   A290, A291
Major, John M.   A292
Mares, Francis H.   E54
Marlowe, Christopher   A36,
   A81, A142, A320, A353,
   B16, B31, B110, B114,
   B124, B151, D51, D140,
   E30
Marotti, Arthur F.   A293,
   A294
Marston, John   A2, A89,
   A214, A270, A366, B55,
   B108, B123, D1, D45,
   D71, D79, D98, D103,
   D115, D123, D126, E30
Martial   D61, D92
Martin, L. C.   E21
Marvell, Andrew   B100
Mason, H. A.   B107
Masque   A31, A93, A96-
   A99, A101, A103, A155,
   A157, A166, A167, A168,
   A170, A221, A272, A273,

A284, A299, A316, A317,
   A324, A427, A431, B23,
   B35, B50, B56, B83,
   B109, B121, B125, D8,
   D24, D31, D33, D46, D64,
   D73, D75, D78, D82,
   D91a, D102, D118, D135,
   E1, E27, E28, E33
Masque of Augurs   A428
Masque of Beauty   A374
Masque of Blackness   A272,
   A273, A372
Masque of Gipsies   E43
Masque of Queens   A155,
   B136, B143
Massinger, Philip   A136,
   A160, A213, B31, B43,
   D3, D103, E45
Matchett, Wm. H.   B108
Maxwell, J. C.   A295-A297
May, Louis F.   A298
Meagher, John Carney   A299,
   B109, D82
Meier, T.   A300
Merchant, Paul   A301
Mercury Vindicated   D74
Mervin, Kathleen M.   D83
Messiaen, Pierre   B110
Middleton, Thomas   A85,
   A184, A261, B55, B70,
   B79, B80, D1, D11, D51,
   D94, D102, D103, D123,
   D139
Miles, Josephine   B111
Miller, Joyce   A302
Miller, Richard Henry   D84
Mills, Lloyd Leslie   A303-
   A305, D85
Milton, John   A148, A187,
   A255, A292, A306, A312,
   A434, A440, B35, B106,
   B134, B161, D20, D51
Miner, Earl   B112
Molière   A277, D124, D134
Molin, Sven Eric   E12
Moloney, Michael F.   A306
Moore, Nancy Ann Newell

D86
Moore, Rayburn S. B113
Morahan, Richard Edward
D87
Morality A8, A110, A159,
A246, B36, B122, B167,
D34, D50, D90
Moran, Josephine Bangs
D88
Moussy, Marcel E55
Muir, Kenneth B114, B171,
E22
Munday, Anthony A215,
A461
Mundhenk, Robert Thomas
D89
Murphy, Avon Jack A307
Murray, W. A. A308,
A309
Murrin, Michael A310
Musgrove, Sidney B115,
E56
Musial, Thomas James
D90
Music A96, A97, A99,
A100, A119, A131, A132,
A166, A376, A377, D130,
E32, E33

Nania, Anthony J. A311
Nash, Ralph A312-A315
Nashe, Th. A390, B114
Nature and art D9
Nelson, Cathryn Anne D91
Nelson, Charles W. D91a
Neoclassicism A50, A219,
B22, B147, B180, D5,
D125
Nevo, Ruth A316
New Inn, The A71, A124,
A138, A190, A237, A263,
A267, A343, B52, B113
Newdigate, Bernard H. E23
Newton, Richard Coleman
D92
Nichols, J. G. B116, D93

Nichols, Mariane D94
Nicholson, Brinsley E24-E26
Nicoll, Allardyce A317,
B117, B117a, E46
Norland, Howard Bernett
B162, D95
Northcote-Bade, Kirsty A318
Nosworthy, J. M. A319,
A320
Noyes, Robert Gale B118

Oates, Mary Irby D96
Oberon, the Fairy Prince
A40, A99, A165, B136,
E44
Obertello, A. E57
O'Connor, Daniel A321
Ode A107, A196, A339,
B106, B148, D96
O'Dell, Jerry Clinton D97
O'Donnell, Norbert F. A322
Old Comedy A108
Olive, W. J. A323, B119
Omans, Stuart E. D98
Oras, Ants B120
Orgel, Stephen A324, B121,
E27, E28
Ornstein, Robert A325-A327,
B85, B122, E29
Osborn, James M. A328
Osgood, Charles G. A329
Overall, Frances Morgan
Bernard D99
Overbury, Sir Thomas B146
Ovid A20, A144, A320

Palmer, Ralph Graham B123
Pan's Anniversary A434
Papajewski, Helmut A330
Parfitt, G. A. E. A331-
A335, D100
Parker, R. B. A336
Parr, Johnstone A337, A338,
B124
Parsons, D. S. J. A339

Partridge, A. C. A340,
A341, B125, B125a, B126,
E29a
Partridge, Edward B.
A342-A345, B127, D101,
E62, E68
Paster, Gail Kern D102
Pastoral A455, B133, D17,
D20, D26
Peery, Wm. A346, A347
Peltz, Catharine W. A348
Pennanen, Esko V. B128,
B129
Perry, George Francis
D103
Peterson, Richard Scot
D104
Petronella, Vincent F.
A349, A350
Phelps, Gilbert B130
Phialas, Peter G. A351
Pineas, Rainer A352
Piper, Wm. B. A353
Plain Style A418, A438,
B170
Pleasure Reconciled to Vir-
tue A221, E35, E42
Plumstead, A. W. A354
Poetaster A148, A173,
A314, A356, A366, A399,
A426, A444, B36b, B95,
D138, E3, E78
Poetry A4, A14, A26,
A140, A310, A331, A333,
A353, A361, A379, A405,
A412, B44, B67, B76,
B82, B96, B107, B111,
B116, B130, B132, B144,
B170, B174, B175, D27,
D35, D40, D42, D47,
D53, D65, D76, D81,
D93, D100, D104, D114,
D127, D135, D137, E4,
E5, E5a, E11, E14,
E15, E16, E18, E19,
E21, E22, E23, E29a,
E35a, E36

Pope, Alexander A463, B81,
B134
Potter, John M. A355
Potter, L. D. D106
Potts, Abbie Findlay A356
Potts, L. J. A357
Praz, Mario B131, E30,
E101
Presley, Horton E. D107
Prose A21, B102, E8, E11,
E36
Puritans D25
Putney, Rufus D. A358,
A359
Puttenham, George B132

Quinn, Edward B133, B137
Quintana, Ricardo E36

Rabkin, Norman B17a
Race, Sidney A360
Rackin, Phyllis A361
Rajan, B. B134
Ralegh, W. A403
Ransom, Shirley Farley
D108
Rathmell, J. C. A. A362
Read, Forrest Godfrey D109
Redding, David C. A363
Redwine, James D., Jr.
A364, B135, D110, E31
Reed, Robert R., Jr. A365,
B136
Reiman, Donald H. A366
Rexroth, Kenneth A367
Reyburn, Marjorie L. A368
Reynolds, Henry B143
Rhetoric A407, A438, A451,
B142, B180, D29, D36,
D59, D117
Rhome, Frances Dodson
D111
Ribner, Irving B137
Rich, Barnaby B138
Ricks, Christopher A369

Riddell, James Allen D112
Riley, Michael Howard D113
Rivers, Isabel D114
Robbins, Martin L. D115
Roberts, S. C. B139
Robinson, E. A. B140
Robinson, James Edward
   A37C D116
Rollin, Roger B. A371
Rollo, Duke of Normandy
   A212, E45
Romains, Jules E102
Roman plays A389, D97,
   D136
Rosenberg, Marvin A372
Rosky, Wm. A373
Ross, Th. W. A374
Rulfs, Donald J. A375
Ryan, A. P. B141

Sabol, Andrew J. A376,
   A377, E32, E33
Sackton, Alexander H.
   A378, A379, B142
Sad Shepherd A322, A437,
   B136, E79
Sakowitz, Alexandre H.
   D117
Sale, Arthur E58, E74,
   E103
Salingar, L. G. A380,
   A381
Salmon, Vivian B143
Sanders, Norman E46
Sansom, Clive B144
Sanvic, Romain B145
Satire A136, A194, A205,
   A229, A271, A283, A354,
   A368, B11, B15a, B43,
   B55, B59, B70, B87,
   B88, B138, B171, D49,
   D71, D97, D108, D121,
   D124, D125, D126
Savage, James E. A382-
   A386, B146
Sawin, Lewis A387

Scaliger A286
Schelling, F. E. B147, E34
Scherer, Hans E85
Scheve, D. A. A388
Schlösser, A. A389
Schlüter, Kurt von B148
Schoenbaum, S. B149, B150,
   B171
Schücking, Levin L. von
   B151
Scoufos, Alice Lyle A390
Sejanus A42, A43, A44,
   A45, A55, A122, A137,
   A163, A179, A185, A200,
   A206, A252, A257, A265,
   A293, A296, A297, A369,
   A410, B7, B36b, B71,
   B119, D36, D50, D87, D113,
   D133, E3, E34, E80-E83
Sellin, Paul R. B152
Seneca A439, B89, B123
Seronsy, Cecil C. A391,
   A392
Seymour-Smith, Martin
   B153, E75
Shaaber, M. A. A394
Shadwell, Th. A363
Shakespeare, William A32,
   A34, A38, A47, A54,
   A94, A126, A129, A134,
   A150, A153, A173, A174,
   A178, A193, A202, A206-
   A208, A211, A235, A242,
   A243, A256, A285, A297,
   A317, A327, A330, A341,
   A351, A356, A360, A372,
   A385, A390, A399, A402,
   A404, A415, A420, A430,
   A432, A442, A457, A458,
   A463, B4, B12, B13,
   B15a, B16, B17a, B21,
   B27, B37, B39, B40,
   B48, B52, B64, B70,
   B74, B98, B108, B115,
   B119, B120, B122, B126,
   B137, B149, B150, B151,
   B155, B161, B166, B171,

B173, B176, B177, B183, D5, D11, D45, D51, D94, D115, D119, D130, D133, D134, D140

Shapiro, I. A. A395

Sharpe, Robert B. A396

Shaw, Bernard A421

Shaw, Catherine Maud D118

Simmonds, James D. D154

Simonini, R. C., Jr. A397, B155

Simpson, Evelyn E9-E11

Simpson, Percy A174, A398-A401, B156, B157, E9-E11

Sirluck, Ernest A402

Sisson, C. J. A403, A404, B158

Skelton, Robin A405

Slater, John Frederick D119

Slights, William W. E. A406, D120

Sloan, Th. O. A407

Snuggs, Henry L. A408, A409

Society A105, A106, A257, B41, B92, B105, D2, D10, D41, D102, D132, D133

Somerset, J. A. B. A410

Soule, Donald Earnest D121

South, Malcolm Hudson A411, D122

Spanos, Wm. V. A412

Spencer, Hazelton E29

Spencer, T. J. B. E35, E42, E44, E46, E47

Spenser, Edmund A33, A68, A84, A90, A126, A329, B68, B100, B161

Sprague, Arthur Colby A413

Stagecraft A6, A336, A410, A413, A445, A462, B47, B118, B143

Stagg, Louis Charles B159, D123

Staple of News, The A220, A238, A259, A303, A338, A385, A440, B71, D86

Starnes, D. T. A414, B160

Starr, G. A. A415

Steane, J. B. E59

Steensma, Robt. C. A416

Steese, Peter A417

Stein, Arnold A418

Stern, Charles Herman D124

Sternfeld, Frederick W. B160a

Stevenson, Warren A420

Stickney, Ruth Frances D125

Stodder, Joseph Henry D126

Stoicism D133

Stokes, E. E., Jr. A421

Stoll, E. E. B161

Stroud, Theodore A. A422

Stroup, Thomas B. E35a

Structure A3, A5, A7, A16, A27, A47, A177, A195, A259, A260, A265, A266, A304, A433, A436, B21, B40, B58, B66, D4, D44, D55, D62, D75, D109, D120, D129, D138

Summers, Jos. H. A423

Swardson, Harold Roland, Jr. D127

Sweeney, James Gerard D128

Swift, Jonathan A205, A392

Swinburne, A. C. B162

Sylvester, Wm. A424

Syme, Ronald B163

Tabachnick, Stephen E. A425

Talbert, Ernest Wm. A426-A428, B160

Tale of a Tub A60, B24, D111, D138, E85

Tannenbaum, Samuel A. and Dorothy R. B164

Targan, Barry Donald A429, D129
Tasis, Rafael E104
Tave, Stuart M. A430
Taylor, Dick, Jr. A431, B165
Taylor, George C. B166
Textual problems A141, A158, A251, A281, A301, A446, B36a, B36b, B62
Thayer, C. G. A432, A433, B167
Thompson, Marvin Orville D130
Thompson, W. L. A434
Thomson, Patricia A435
Thron, E. M. A436
Tiedje, Egon B168
Timber see Discoveries
Timings, E. K. A33
"To Penshurst" A92, A120, A188, A198, A269, A362, A456, D12
Tourneur, Cyril A325, A380, B110, B122, D1, D123, E30
Townsend, Freda L. A437, B169
Tragedy A56, A63, A112, A265, A315, A439, A443, B151, B152, B159
Tragicomedy B69, D24
Tribe of Ben A64, B25, B33, B112, D23, E29a
Trimpi, Wesley A418, A438, B170

Underwood D63
Ure, Peter A439, A440, B171
Usury A10

Valian, Maxine Kent D131
Van den Berg, Sara Streich D132

Van Deusen, Marshall A441
Vaughan, Henry B154
Vawter, Marvin L. D133
Velz, John W. A442
Villiers, Jacob I. de A443
Virtue D104
Vision of Delight A191
Volpone A7, A9, A12, A19, A46, A49, A75, A77, A82, A87, A88, A100, A108, A110, A115, A116, A121, A130, A151, A159, A164, A182-A184, A186, A189, A192, A201, A254, A257, A262, A264, A266, A302, A304, A313, A325, A326, A335, A352, A375, A378, A380, A388, A392, A411, A453, B7, B10, B32, B53, B71, B88, B103, B133, B160a, B177, D36, D54, D71, D83, D119, E3, E17, E24, E34, E86-E106

Wada, Yuichi B172
Waith, Eugene M. A444-A446, E63
Walker, Ellen Louise D134
Walker, Ralph S. A447, A448, E40
Wallerstein, Ruth C. E36
Wallis, Lawrence B. B173
Walton, Geoffrey B86, B174, B175
Warr, Nancy Nairn D135
Warren, Michael John A449, D136
Watson, Elizabeth A450
Watson, Geo. A451, B102
Watson, Th. L. A452
Webster, John A420, B110, B151, D1, D103, D123, E30
Weimann, Robt. B176
Weld, John S. A453
Wells, Stanley B177, E47

165